# Do You Remember?

# DO YOU REMEMBER?

## *Bungay, a Gracious Town*

*by*

**IRIS REEVE**

with best wishes
Iris Reeve.

Morrow & Co.
Bungay, Suffolk
1994

First published by Morrow & Co., Bungay Suffolk 1994





ISBN 0 948903 15 5

Typeset in Bungay by PDQ Repro
Printed and bound by The Ipswich Book Company

This book is dedicated to my five children,
in love and gratitude for all the happiness
they have given me.

# CONTENTS

# PREFACE

I am always full of gratitude that so much of my life has been spent in our lovely Suffolk countryside, where every season has something new to offer. The games season of bowling hoops, spinning tops, marbles, and skipping; then, picking primroses in Shoe Devil Lane, gathering acorns and blackberries, paddling in the Train Bridge river, gleaning corn, and, perhaps happiest of all, trundling a barrow to find holly – holly with many berries and one special piece to stick in the Christmas pudding. St. Valentine's Eve, and Guy Fawkes, and carol singing. There was always something to look forward to, and, even in childhood, a happy looking back.

"Let's go and get primroses, remember the lovely ones we gathered last year? Near that stream. There were tadpoles and little frogs. Do you remember – ?"

## CHAPTER ONE

# Bungay, a Gracious Town

Bungay was a gracious town as I remember it just before the First World War. The streets were wide and clean, tree-lined and pleasant, and always busy – busy with horse-drawn traffic. The slow rhythmic clop, clop, of the horses lifting their shaggy feet as they drew laden carts which had been filled from standing trucks in the 'goods' station. There was music in the unhurrying step of the horses. The driver might jerk them to a standstill with a "Whoa there!" as he stopped to call to an acquaintance on the pavement, "Good day to you  Missus. Nice day again". The horses, not loth to stop awhile, shook their heads and their shiny brasses jingled. Yes, even the carthorses which drew coal had their harness polished brightly, and their dark brown coats shone with health and good grooming. Smaller ponies would pull the baker's carts and the milk carts. Bread was unwrapped and warm and crusty. The penny buns had big juicy currants. I wonder why they are small and hard as pebbles nowadays?

The bread was made and baked in the bake-house behind the shop. Children loved to see the baker pounding and rolling the white dough, and then putting it in the rows and rows of square tins waiting to be filled. The tins were put in a long, cupboard like oven, and pushed to the back with a kind of flat metal scoop with a long handle.

Housewives from the houses nearby brought their cakes and pies and tins of buns, even a dish of pig's fry and onions, to be baked in the big oven at the cost of one penny. This was especially useful in the summer when heating the wall oven in the small cottage kitchens made them oppressively hot.

The milkman brought the milk in big, shiny, well-scoured steel containers and measured out pints and half pints into the jugs of their customers. It is incredible to realise how short a time it is since milk was brought in this way. Even after the Second World War, our milkman arrived in a cart pulled by his mare, Peggy, beloved of my small children. When I first married, seven different 'cow-keepers' delivered milk in Southend Road. They all seemed to make a living and the milk was always fresh and creamy. Now only two vendors come here, and only once a day.

An equal number of greengrocers' carts called, including one very old vendor, who pushed his wares on a handcart; and the postman delivered letters three times a day. There were fish-carts, too, and the housewife could buy herrings or sprats or a nice piece of cod fresh from the Lowestoft market. I remember old Mr. Ward pushing his laden barrow up the road, calling "Blow-ters, red herring, fresh blow-ters". Fresh, very nourishing, and cheap at two for three ha'pence. He used to say when he arrived breathless at the gate, "Bless me, Ma'am, that ole road grow steeper every time I come up it!"

Now, as I grow old, I realise the truth in his words. The slight incline in the road has indeed become rougher and steeper. It is no longer worn by feet bringing provender to the housewife, as in the old days. Apart from the two milk vans, a coal lorry is occasionally seen, or the post office van, and a big tanker bringing oil to houses with central heating.

It is many years since I have seen in the road, a greengrocer's cart with its colourful display of oranges and red apples, pink tulips and bright daffodils, the magic country smell of cabbages and swedes and celery. A child hopping hopefully near the rosy pile of apples would probably have one tossed to him, with a careless "Like an apple, ole partner? Here, catch!"

The sourpuss might say that doubtless the greengrocer weighed his fingers in the next pound of fruit to make up for his good deed. But who cares? The child was happy:

'He who gives a child a treat
Makes joy bells ring in Heaven's street'.

Of the vendors of fish, some carried shrimps, or cockles and mussels in baskets on their heads.

There was old Mr. Alborough (possibly old only in a child's eyes). He was very tall and slim, and he moved along with the swinging gait of a sailor. Hands in pockets, he cried his wares, "Shrimps- shr- - imps". Doors would open on each side of the street. "I'll have some of your shrimps Mr. Alborough. What are they today?"

"Penny a pint, m'dear, same as yesterday". He would lift the basket down to the pavement and measure out the shrimps with a half-pint earthenware mug. Then, half stooping, he would lift the basket to his head again, and carry on along the street, often taking the middle of the road, for there was no fear of a car tearing round the corner to upset him and his load of shrimps.

The streets were often thick with dust in dry weather, especially in the summer. Our leather boots, neatly polished when we left home, were grey with dust before school was reached. It took but a second to rub the toe of one's boots against the back of a woollen stockinged leg, and so march into school with shining toe caps and dust covered grey heels.

The water cart, horse-drawn of course, was driven through the streets sending a silver spray of water to 'lay the dust'. The water cart was always followed by a delighted crowd of children. Sometimes the driver would press whatever it was that regulated the spray, and send a heightened shower over the nearest children. To their great delight indeed, for it was refreshing as well as exciting to be splashed on a hot day. Those were not the days of scanty summer clothing, mini-skirts, bare legs, and sandals. Long woollen stockings and leather lace-up or button boots, at least one petticoat under the just-below-knee-length dress, which, although it might be of cotton in summer, had long sleeves and was buttoned to the neck. The boys, too, had their serge jackets and waistcoats and knickerbockers, and round hard collars. Yet they raced over the Common, and jumped dykes and played 'leap-frog' and hop-scotch in the streets, bowled hoops and climbed trees. Despite the restrictive and uncomfortable clothing, childhood was a time for running and laughing.

But where has all the laughter and running gone? I often wonder when I see small children walking soberly home from school. Is the energy sapped by spending too much time hunched in front of a television screen in a centrally heated room, with the movement of air restricted by double-glazing? Has the running and laughing gone with the March dust, which countrymen said was worth a guinea a bushel?

When we were young there was no need of television, for every season brought its own delight. Marble time, when almost every child had his or her bag of small, gaily coloured clay marbles, bought for a penny a dozen. In those days of limited pocket money, it was heartrending to have to choose between a ha'penny of marbles or an ounce of mixed sweets. There were also the more expensive and highly cherished glass marbles with their kaleidoscope of rainbow colours, and the plain glass stopper from ginger-beer bottles, known as 'alleys'.

"You are to come straight home from school", ordered our mothers; but the 'straight home' must have often taken a very long time. All the way from school to home, games of marbles were in progress. The marbles were bowled along the gutter at the side of the pavement, and when two marbles were within spanning distance, the small hand was stretched to span the marbles and so win the game. Then, suddenly, marbles all disappeared, and hoops or skipping-ropes or tops would have their day. Plain wooden spinning-tops cost a ha'penny, and their owners often chalked a design on top to make it 'look lovely', as it was whipped around. The whips were made from a length of string from Mama's string drawer, tied to a stick cut from the hedge. Oh, to hear again that satisfying 'ping' as the top was whipped expertly on its neck and sent flying twenty five yards down the street.

As well as tops and marbles, and the always unfinished games of hop-scotch, there were other delights to lengthen the homeward journey. As children came out from school in the dusk of a winter's afternoon, the lamplighter was starting his round of lighting the gas lamps in the streets. He had a long stick, like a crook with which he deftly pulled a chain to ignite the mantle in its glass container. He was always followed by a crowd of children for his lighting stick seemed to hold as much magic for them as the flute of the Pied Piper had done for the children of Hamelin. As the stick touched the lamp, all the young faces turned up to look, and if the lamp did not ignite immediately, you could feel the tension of indrawn breath; and then the delighted "O – O – Oh", as, with a sharp click, the light came on, and sent its scanty ray across the darkening street. Then the firm plodding step of the lamplighter on the pavement, and the trotting steps of the children around him, hurrying along to the next lamp.

The Town Crier was another great favourite. There was one called 'Old Jack'. He never hurried over his task, but plodded with heavy strides, from one stopping place to another, and would frequently pause awhile to take a 'wad o' tobacco' from his pocket, and chew it, he said, to clear his voice. He would slowly ring the heavy hand bell, and with a loud "Take public notice", deliver his message. Doors opened on each side of the street, and children ran swiftly home, for they could be rewarded with an apple or a piece of freshly baked shortcake, if they delivered their parents a piece of news before it had reached their neighbours.

Another visitor to send the young feet scurrying homeward was the 'Windmill man', or the 'Jamjar Man'. He pushed a handcart, set round with toy windmills, made of stiff paper on the end of a stick, which would twirl merrily if you ran fast on a windy day. These windmills were given in exchange for a jamjar, so mothers were entreated – "Mama, give us a jamjar quick". They were not always readily given, because most housewives made their own jam, and needed whatever jars they could get. Homemade jam was of course much cheaper to produce, and many housewives were suspicious of shop jam. "Just plum skin and water', they would say; or "Raspberry juice and chips of wood to look like pips".

'Old Jack' was also something of a fortune teller. "What will I be when I grow up?" a child would ask him. Jack would stand and scratch his head, then reply, "What do you want to be?".

"Oh, a school teacher".

"Tha's right, you set your heart to that, and that's what you'll be".

"What will I be, Jack?", piped up another child.

"What do you want to be, ole partner?"

"I don't know".

"Well, there's plenty of don't knows, but I don't doubt you'll find something to do, same as the rest", the old man would retort.

One of the greatest joys of childhood was the circus procession. Three or four times a year a circus would visit the town, and erect its 'Big Top' on the Little Common (now taken over by the Printing Works buildings), or on the Fair Meadow off St. John's Road. At twelve o'clock on the day of the circus just as morning school finished, the Procession began. It was usually led by a band which signalled the start by energetic banging of the big drum. Circus ladies stood fantastically on the backs of their delightful ponies, looking almost as glamorous in their spangled costumes as they did in the harsh lighting of the circus tent at night.

From the Common, along Station Road (Outney Road), and up Earsham Street to the Market Place. Along St. Mary's Street and Upper Olland Street, and Bardolph Road, across Lower Olland Street and into Trinity Street, Broad Street, and back to the Common. The drums beat and the clowns danced along in the middle of the road; children thronged the pavements and errand boys leaned on their bicycles. Grocers and butchers and bakers stood at their shop doors, enjoying the sight, until the sound of the drums and the excited shouts of the children faded into the distance. Then, looking a bit shame-faced they would call to the errand boys "Hurry up with them orders now! Can't be standing about here all day".

Whether or not the circuses were of a high standard I did not know, but to children and I think to the parents also, the two or three hours of the performances was time spent in an unforgettable wonderland, of glittering tinsel, jumping ponies, trumpeting elephants, and ridiculous clowns, and the warm circus smell of gas flares, and sawdust, and animals.

Another frequent visitor to the town was the Organ Grinder. He had a small monkey sitting on top of the organ, scratching himself, and turning his tiny head from side to side, looking at the children with inquisitive sad eyes. He held out a tin cup for the scanty ha'pence which we threw to him.

I like to think that the monkey was happy, as

he climbed onto the top of the barrel organ, chacking in his strange, wise way. I am sure his owner was kind. He tucked him warmly under his arm, as they moved from street to street.

There was another monkey in the town. It belonged to Mr. Inwards, who had the baker's shop opposite the Roman Catholic School which I attended. On rare occasions, this monkey would climb onto the roof of the shop, and would gambol along, perilously near the edge, picking the pieces of moss from the roof, and throwing them to the pavement below. The owner would bring a long ladder and climb up to fetch him down. That was another pantomime, because the monkey did not want to be fetched; but eventually he would be enticed to jump onto his master's shoulder, and cling on while they both descended to the street again.

There seemed to be much heavier falls of snow in winters then. The snow plough was out frequently. It was drawn by two horses and moved slowly along, pushing the snow into what seemed to us, mountainous heaps on each side of the road. It delighted the children to climb on these heaps, and probably sink deep into the soft white snow which never seemed cold or wet! There were no rubber or Wellington boots then, except for the thick rubber knee-boots or waders, worn by fishermen, or by the men clearing dykes on the Common. Thick leather boots, and woollen stockings outside, and wholesome food inside seemed protection enough. The common cold did not seem to be the everyday irritation it has increasingly become now.

One or two gentlemen had horse-drawn sleighs. It seemed to my young eyes the height of luxury – the beautiful, high-stepping horses, their harnesses jingling in the cold air, the shining runners of the sleigh, and the proud owner wrapped warmly with a skin rug over his knees, holding the reins in gloved hands. So did the Snow Queen ride, with the ice-enchanted Gerda beside her. And so would I ride one day when I was grown up. For, to a child, grownupness is the key that opens the gate to the boundless time when you can do all you want to do.

Alas, the beautiful high-stepping horses are gone, and the snow, when there is any, no longer has its white, virgin purity, but becomes dirty and degraded as it is shovelled on to a lorry and taken away.

And if there was more snow in winter, was there not more, and hotter sunshine in summer? When the snow-balling had finished, and the sliding on the frozen flood water on the Common was done, and the flood water had drained back, and the narrow river flowed calmly again under the rickety wooden bridges, then came Spring. Spring, with its glory of shining marsh-marigolds, and cuckoo flowers, and forget-me-nots on the river bank. When the dykes were alive with frogs and tadpoles, and little darting tiddlers; and at last we could go across the Common, past old Mr Baldry's house, and climb the slope up to Bath Hills.

Bath Hills is really in Ditchingham on the Norfolk side of the Waveney, but it always seemed to us part of the Common, and therefore part of Bungay. Even in late Spring the Common was boggy still, and the wooded lane along the top of Bath Hills was thick with mud through which we slithered and slipped, or climbed up on to the nearest banks to negotiate the most difficult parts. We were determined to reach Target Hill, a narrow clearing that led very steeply down to the river again. Here primroses grew, and hundreds of tiny black spiders ran in and out of the primrose tufts. The grass was warm, and the clean scent of the flowers and the dank minty smell of the river seemed like Paradise.

The first visit to Target Hill, the first gathered bunch of primroses was, to we children, the beginning of the long, delightful summer days.

There was magic in going out to play after tea, if only for half an hour. And the games we played – are they all forgotten? 'Grandmother's Steps', and 'French Touch', and the favourite, 'My Sheep, My Sheep, Come Home'. The 'Mother Sheep' standing on the soft grass, about fifty yards from the 'Wolf', crouched behind the gorse bush. The rest of us huddled in a group between the two. The Mother Sheep called out:

"My sheep, my sheep, come home".

And the other sheep would call back: "We're afraid".

"Afraid of what?"

"The Wolf".

"The Wolf is gone to Devonshire, and won't come back for many a year. My sheep, my sheep come home".

Then the mad rush over the springy turf to reach the safety of the Mother Sheep, before the Wolf, darting out from his hiding place, caught as many of us as possible.

CHAPTER TWO

# Bungay Shops

Apart from the continuous rumbling of heavy traffic, St. Mary's Street has changed little since the early part of this century. I stand by the War Memorial and look across the street, and see the shops as they were over seventy years ago.

Next to the lane leading to the 'Back o' the Hills' was a chemist's shop. It seemed small and dark because the shelves in the windows at each side of the doors were laden with bottles and jars. In particular, I remember some enormous dark blue and dark green jars catching the light from outside and yet seeming to hold a depth of darkness too. Children said that these jars were filled with poison! Nowadays when chemists' shops stock so many different commodities – handbags, baskets, cameras and sunglasses, records and baby clothes, it is difficult to realise the mysterious atmosphere of a small rather gloomy shop that dealt almost exclusively in medicines and lotions, and on a shelf high up, close to the ceiling, was another row of dark blue and dark green 'poison' bottles.

To enter the shop you opened a narrow door between the display windows. A bell tinkled and you stood a little fearfully inside the door. There might be a slight movement of a curtain that hid the back part of the shop, and behind which the proprietor dispensed his medicines. He was a slightly built, ascetic looking man with thinning sandy hair and very kind blue eyes, behind rimless glasses. Perhaps you had gone in with a prescription and would hand him a scrap of paper on which the doctor had scribbled something in Chinese or double Dutch. The chemist read this apparently without difficulty and said mildly "Did you bring a bottle? Will you wait or call again in about ten minutes?"

Of course you preferred to wait – to breathe in the fragrant perfumes of many kinds of soap and baby powder, interlaced with cinnamon and peppermint and liquorice, all wrapped in that slightly fearful atmosphere of alchemy. Yes, although a call at the chemist's was often for unpleasant things like liquorice powder and syrup of figs, and 'sick' lozenges, you preferred to wait.

Next door to the chemist's shop was a draper and milliner's premises (now the chemist's shop of R. McDaniel Ltd.). This was a large establishment but it was so full of merchandise that the floor space for customers was small. Just inside the door stood rolls of shiny linoleum and piles of thick coconut matting and fibre doormats. On the shelves were bales of material ranging from grey (unbleached) calico, and gaily flowered cotton prints, to the thicker dress materials and the bright printed cretonnes for furnishing. The proprietor did not serve the customers, but handed them over to one of his young lady assistants standing behind the counters on either side in neat black dresses. He would welcome his customers with a bland smile, and was as polite to a child coming in for a 'knot of tape' , as he was to some adult ordering 'morning aprons' for all their domestic staff.

It was delightful to visit this shop with Mama because then you could wriggle on to one of the round seated wooden chairs that stood by the counter, and sit contentedly watching while Mama carried on the business of buying white cotton material for summer chemises, or whatever else she had come in to look at. The shop smelled of new materials – the sharp, rather acrid smell of stiff cotton, and the softer warm smell of red flannel and the strange rather mildewy odour of linoleum and matting.

"Show this lady some white calico, Miss Brown", the proprietor would say to one of the assistants, probably fresh from school, barely fourteen years old, and blushing rosily at being addressed as 'Miss'. These girls were somewhat unkindly called 'calico-renders' by other school leavers who went into domestic service or some other career.

"Was it calico for chemises Ma'am?", she would ask. "We have a strong bleached one for six-three (sixpence three farthings), or a fine madapolan at eight three, and there's a very soft nainsook for best wear at ten three a yard". Mama would feel the materials between finger and thumb. "There's a lot of 'dress' in this one", she might say, or "this one is much too thin". The material decided upon, the assistant measured each yard with a long round yard stick, unrolling the material from the bale. Then there would be narrow cotton lace for the neck edging, and I would probably whisper loudly "Are they for me? Can I have baby ribbon threaded through mine?"

The bill would be given to the proprietor for checking and then the money was taken to a till further down the shop. This was only a drawer with separate compartments for coppers and silver and probably banknotes.

"Thank you Ma'am, that will be a farthing out (change). Will you have a farthing out or a packet of pins?"

"Is there anything more I can do for you?", the proprietor would ask. "Yes, I was thinking of getting my little girl a new summer hat", Mama might reply; and I wanted to hop up and down in delight but dare not, lest Mama thought I was behaving badly and decided against the new hat.

"The millinery department", said the proprietor. "Follow me. This way". And he would go ahead, swaying a little jauntily, the gold watch chain across his waistcoat jingling, to the far end of the shop, where two shallow steps led up to the millinery room. Here the senior milliner and her two apprentices sat sewing busily. There were pretty things to see here, pieces of coloured net and soft tulle, velvet ribbons and sprays of artificial flowers. There were hatpins, too, with glass tops that sparkled in the light like jewels; and, of course, the hats, on small stands, looking rather strange with no faces under their brims.

"Children's hats, Madam? Yes, we had a fresh lot in this morning". The milliner would lift a large, round cardboard box to the glass counter and bring out hats wrapped in layers of tissue paper, that sounded mysterious and whispering like its name.

Although the milliner herself created many of the hats for her adult customers, children's hats were much of a muchness – white or cream coloured straw, with a band of ribbon, or a wreath of artificial flowers. Some of them had ribbons to tie under the chin, but were usually kept on by white elastic.

Carrying the precious hat-box, I skipped home happily with my mother. But there was an unfortunate sequel to this shopping expedition. I was so anxious to try on my new hat, that I could not wait to go upstairs, but climbed onto the fender in the sitting-room to admire it in the mirror over the mantlepiece. Clumsily in my haste, I knocked down a precious Venetian glass vase on the mantlepiece. Vanity of Vanities. I was not allowed to wear the new hat for several Sundays to come.

In memory I always see this shop in a haze of sunshine, with the sun's rays streaming through the window, and making rainbow lights on the glass counter. There must have been *some* wet days, but perhaps at that time when the busy housewife could not spare the time for shopping everyday, she could choose a sunny day for going out.

I often wonder how a housewife managed to get through all the chores she had. There would certainly have been no time for watching television even late in the evening. Water had to be fetched from an outside pump and could be used only in small quantities for washing-up, filling the copper, filling the zinc bath. Then all the dirty water had to be taken out and emptied instead of gurgling joyfully down the drain at the lifting of a plug. Lamps had to be cleaned and refilled with oil, and candlesticks polished. It is no easy matter to scrape congealed tallow from metal candlesticks, or to polish a glass lamp chimney which has been blackened with smoke. Coal fires made a lot of dust, and the kitchen range had to be polished with black lead to give it that fine silvery sheen that most of them had. A kitchen range was such a happy thing in the winter, with the purr of the steaming kettle and always something bubbling in a saucepan giving out a warm appetising smell. It was probably bone broth with every kind of vegetable obtainable. There might be an earthenware jar of stewed pears flavoured with cloves. Porridge was made overnight and boiled up again ready for breakfast. There was none of this 'ready-brek', or instant coffee which is used today. Perhaps one loses some of the happy anticipation in the preparation of a meal.

Next to the draper's shop was a small one

with, above the entrance door, a large black hat. This shop was a hatter's, hosier's and haberdasher's, and the small windows at each side of the door showed discreetly coloured ties and socks and large white handkerchiefs. I particularly liked this shop because it was so much like the picture in my Nursery Rhyme book of the establishment to which Mother Hubbard hurried to buy her dog a hat:–

"She went to the Hatter's to buy him a hat,
But when she came home, he was chasing
the cat".

We used to go to this shop to buy Dadda a tie for a birthday or Christmas present. Two ladies, the daughters of the owner of the shop, served here. They were small and gentle and sweet, and very anxious to please in a head on one side, birdlike, fashion.They wore identical white blouses, with narrow lace at the wrists, and a ruching of lace at the neck. One of the Misses Roper would say, archly, her eyes almost disappearing in a screwed up smile "A blue tie? or perhaps a brarn. Is it for a *young* gentleman, or (her voice dropping politely), an *elderly* gentleman?"

"It's for my Dadda, and he likes blue".

"Well, I think *blue* is more suitable for a *young* gentleman, but you can return it if it does not please him. This one is very pretty at one and a penny three, perhaps a trifle *young*? Is there anything more? A useful handkerchief? Warm socks?" Then her hands would flutter over a sheet of brown paper (no stuffing things into paper bags). The purchase was made into a neat parcel slowly and carefully and tied with string. A loop was made so it could be carried on one's finger. No gay, holly-sprigged paper or sticky sellotape.

As we left and closed the door, a bell tinkled a goodbye, just as it tinkled a welcome when one entered the shop. Some of the bells were loud and clanged noisily for some seconds after you entered, and gave a feeling of guilt, especially on a warm summer afternoon, as if one had disturbed a quietly resting shopkeeper. Indeed, there was an old shoemaker in Bridge Street who always came to the counter at the call of his jangling bell, saying "Hello, hello, young lady. I do believe I was asleep. Been waiting long?"

Further along St. Mary's Street was an ironmonger's shop. It is still an ironmongers and still called by the older Bungay people, 'Bowtells'. It was quite small and so full of merchandise that it seemed even smaller. A step led up from the street, and the windows on each side were almost obscured by hanging galvanised baths. The space inside was very restricted. A stride took you from the door to the counter, and everywhere was taken up with goods for sale. Baths and buckets and watering-cans hung from the ceiling, and bails of string and bundles of bass spread over the counter. The only touch of brighter colour came from packets of seeds with their gay flower pictures – candytuft and orange nasturtiums and purple and yellow pansies. There was an exhilarating smell of paraffin, and the earthiness of seed potatoes and the straw fragrance of bass. This Dadda used for tying up his flowers, and I used to beg some from him to make little straw hats for my dolls. There was only straw coloured bass then, not even green, and certainly nothing like the great variety of brightly coloured raffia and plastic string which can now be bought.

Sometimes, if a customer asked for something which was not displayed in the shop, one of the assistants would lift a trap-door in the floor behind the counter and call down.

"Jack, bring up a packet of them taller (tallow) candles". A few minutes later, a head and shoulder would appear, and the desired article would be handed over. Sometimes one assistant would mount a narrow staircase in the wall behind the counter and disappear to the floor above. His footsteps overhead – thud, thud, thud – sounded quite alarming, and the single gas jet that hung from the ceiling swayed madly, casting eerie shadows from dark corners, or suddenly illuminating a display of oil-lamps with their glass chimneys and brass and white earthenware bowls.

Indeed, on a winter's afternoon when darkness sets in early, and the gas lamps seemed to emphasise rather than relieve the gloom, shopping was exciting in a rather frightening way. It is difficult to visualise this small crowded space compared with the shop as it is today, reaching all the way from St. Mary's Street to Castle Lane.

Next to the ironmonger's was a grocery store;

and perhaps this was one of the most satisfying of all the shops to visit, especially on a winter's afternoon, when you had thoughts of hot buttered toast for tea. There was the smell of good cheddar cheese and bacon, and tea in wooden chests lined with crackling lead paper that made me think of newly mown hay. Just before and just after Christmas there was the nose-wrinkling tang of oranges. They were usually only available for about six weeks, and the smell of them brought Christmas very near. There was always an orange in the toe of our Christmas stockings, and a stiff new handkerchief.

Large square biscuit tins were neatly stacked on the floor in front of the counters. These tins had glass lids so you could see what was in them. The names of the biscuits were printed on the outside of the tins – 'Nice', 'Petit Beurre', 'Osborne', 'Custard Creams', 'Ginger Nut'. The grocer took a paper bag and followed the customer as she chose the biscuits she wanted, and was very patient and seemingly unperturbed if she was a long time in making up her mind. Everything had to be weighed up, for there were none of today's hygienically wrapped packets and cellophane covered boxes. Currants, sugar, rice, everything was loose, in sacks, tins or other large containers. You could choose from several varieties of rice and dried fruit and even granulated sugar had various degrees of whiteness.

The shop manager and his assistants wore white aprons and although they had to handle much of what was purchased, there seemed to be few of the tummy upsets one hears of now. The assistant would take a handkerchief-sized square of thick blue paper, twist it deftly into a 'bag', and in it he would pour the currants, rice, oatmeal or whatever he had weighed out, firmly fold in the top of the package, and press it down with finger and thumb. The contents never seemed to spill out in the shopping basket on the way home.

There were several harness makers and saddlers shops. The doors of these were hung with horse collars and their shining brasses. The good rich smell of leather spread out into the street. On display were steel curry combs and brushes and the bright blue and red and yellow braid that was twisted to decorate horses' manes on special occasions. One such saddlers' shop stood behind the Corn Merchant's in Cross Street. In the Corn Merchant's shop were sacks of maize, oats and bran and something called 'supers'. It was a large shop and the far end stretched to a hazy distance obscured by the barley scented dust that clouded the air. Almost every householder who had a medium sized garden or yard kept chickens or rabbits, and here we bought a half stone of maize or wheat or bran to feed the rabbits. The 'supers' was like a very thin bran and was mixed with a warm 'mash' for the hens' breakfast.

There were some enormous scales and to these were wheeled sacks of corn on a trolley. There was an old, old man with a dust coloured beard and a cap pushed back on his dust coloured hair. His clothes were dust coloured too. I think if anybody patted him on the back a cloud of dust would have arisen to roll with the rest of the grain dust to the misty end of the shop.

This old man would tug and manoeuvre the sacks off the trolley and untie the string that fastened the corners of the sacks. "Half a stone of maize is it Old Partner? Well just take hold of the bag" – handing over a strong brown paper bag. "Go on, hold it open". He would dip a metal scoop into the bag and pour a rattling cascade of orange coloured maize into the bag and then place it on the scales to weigh it. "Seven pounds exactly. Don't you spill none of that on your way home, do your father 'ull say I give him short measure".

Almost outside the shopping area, in Lower Olland Street there was a tiny shop which was really the front room of a cottage with a counter down the centre. The small window was always crowded with merchandise and what light there was came in by the cottage door which was usually open. It sold all kinds of sweets, some in glass jars, some in white cardboard boxes, edged with paper lace. There were brandy balls, aniseed balls, jolliboy toffees, caramels, coconut kisses, acid drops and just brightly coloured sticky mixtures. Hanging up like bootlaces were strings of black liquorice, and laid out on dishes among these sweet things were fish. There were red herrings, bloaters and kippers, and sometimes a shimmering heap of silver scaled sprats.

Their wet sightless eyes seemed to blink in the stray beams of sun that caught a dim light from the glass sweet jars.

The fish were loose, and the sweets were weighed out loose, and the same hand that had just put a pair of bloaters in a newspaper for a customer would next be placed in the jar for somebody requesting sweets. So it was not unusual to find fish scales adhering to acid drops or cough lozenges.

In this shop could be found at certain times of the year, two delicacies that are almost unheard of now – tiger nuts and locust beans. These latter were flat and brown, looking like pieces of dried up leather. Sometimes their taste too, reminded me of hard dried up leather, but when at their perfect time of ripeness, they could be really delicious, brittle and chewy and tasting of honey. The tiger nuts, too, were sometimes hard and tasteless like something left over in a cupboard long forgotten; but at other times sweet enough to delight the sweetest tooth.

Also in this shop were small three cornered bags of white or pink sherbert. This could be shaken out and made into a frothy drink, or licked dry giving an exciting sharp tingling to the tongue. Sealing the top of these bags was a wooden whistle which had a small rubber bladder at the end. When blown, the whistle made an unearthly whine as the bladder inflated to egg size, and immediately deflated with an even more unearthly shriek.

Large gaily coloured balloons were not known when we were children. The first of these I saw was an enormous bunch held on a stick by a seaside vendor, who was selling them at twopence each. And to spend a precious twopence on something that the sea breeze could steal from your hand or which could burst into nothingness in a second was beyond the scope of our scanty pocket money. But I remember how beautiful was that bunch of red and blue and orange balloons – as happy as the yellow sand and the summer sky and the shimmering dancing sea. How I envied that Balloon Man his colourful burden.

There were several toy shops, but the rather small but crowded windows – some with leaded panes – did not give a very good view of the goods for sale. There were wooden spinning tops, and bowls of marbles, wooden Dutch dolls and tiny dolls with china heads, hard blue painted eyes, long golden hair and sawdust bodies. These were sold at one penny each; the wooden Dutch dolls could be as much as ninepence. They had painted slits for eyes and black painted tops for hair. What their attraction was I cannot say, but we loved them. I have seen similar dolls with their bright paint quite faded selling in antique shops for as much as thirty pounds. The big 'double-jointed' dolls with eyes that opened and shut, and red parted lips showing tiny white teeth, and 'real' curly hair were beyond the reach of most little girls. They were not only expensive, but their pretty painted china faces broke so easily. Can one ever forget the heartbreak of picking up a loved doll that had fallen flat on its face, and finding ugly jagged cracks and a gaping hole where its pretty face used to be?

Wax dolls were very beautiful, their complexions so exquisitely pink and white and loveably soft. They did not break easily but had to be kept from the heat of the sun or fire. I had one of these wax dolls. It was small and dainty, perhaps nine inches long. My sister had just made it a new pale mauve dress and bonnet. I cuddled it close in my arms. But my mischievous older brother put poor dolly in the oven of the cooking range – just for a minute – just for a lark – and then, forgetting all about it, went off to play. When the oven door was opened later on, there on the the top shelf was dolly's pretty new outfit, floating in a pool of grease.

'Jack in the Boxes' were a great favourite, and wooden monkeys on sticks, and thick earthenware tea-sets. There was not the great variety of cuddly toys one sees now – plush dogs and cats and adorable black and white pandas, and the various characters made famous by television series and comics. Teddies in those days were yellow and hard, with small black 'boot-button' eyes and arms and legs attached with thick, hard wire and loosened easily. There were small clockwork trains that were quickly overwound, and the wire uncoiled with a harsh, unhappy 'whirr': then the anguished cry from the owner "It won't wind up."

There were books with glossy board covers showing an attractive picture of the characters in the stories. These had no paper dust-jackets, but were strong and well made, and lasted through many years of family reading.

Shop window displays were not re-arranged very frequently, so if there was a book you would dearly like to have, it would probably still be there when your birthday came round; or, – a very rare happening – a visiting relative might give you enough money to buy it. We had presents for birthdays and at Christmas time, and perhaps a small gift at Easter or on St. Valentine's Day. My birthday comes in the middle of the year. If I saw something in the window just after Christmas, I had a long time to wait, hoping it would remain unsold.

There was one such book I saw when I was about eight years old, entitled simply 'Fairy Tales', but the picture on the shiny cover was much more alluring than the title of the book. A wolf stood on his hind legs at the front door of a most attractive rose-wreathed country cottage. One paw was lifted to the knocker, and the wolf's head was turned towards the cottage window from which a number of white kids were peeping fearfully. The wolf was no doubt meant to look wickedly cunning, but in fact he was more like an amiable collie dog. The story of the 'Wolf and the Seven Little Kids' I knew well, and probably had heard all the other stories in the book, but I wanted it so much. Every day for weeks I went to the shop window, dreading to find that 'my book' had gone; but it stayed there until my mother bought it for my birthday. It was read and reread, and eventually my own children had it, still in reasonably good condition. They, too, enjoyed 'Hop O' My Thumb', 'The Twelve Dancing

Princesses', and, of course, the wicked wolf who was, in the end, outwitted by the cleverness of the Mother Goat.

When the great 'out of doors' was uninviting in wintry or wet weather we made our own entertainment. As a family we were great readers, and could all read at an early age. We also enjoyed board games 'Snakes and Ladders', 'Ludo' and the rest. We had a race game – a board with a pictured race course, and little metal horses and jockeys. This we played on and on, and in childhood, everything becomes so real. It was not just cardboard with jumps marked out, but a *real* racecourse with horses jumping and falling, and all the excitement of the real thing.

## CHAPTER THREE

# The Sabbath

But when Sunday came, the games had to stop for none were allowed on the Sabbath. Tops and hoops and marbles were put away in the cupboard on Saturday evening to stay there until Monday morning. Sunday was a special day, set apart from the rough and tumble of working day life. A day for going to church and for all the family to take a long walk together in the afternoons in winter, and the evenings in summer.

All the places of worship were well attended. The Roman Catholic church, the Parish church of St. Mary, Holy Trinity. Both these latter were Anglican, but had wide differences in their interpretation of Anglicanism. St. Mary's was considered 'Low' church. Holy Trinity was 'High' because candles were burned on the altar, and a great deal of genuflecting took place. "All that bowing and scraping, you might as well be Catholic and be done with it", muttered the 'Low' church folk; while the 'High' church advocates retorted "No candles! You might as well go to Chapel". For you either belonged to Trinity or St. Mary's and between the two there was a great gulf. This appears strange now there is such a movement towards unity of all denominations. However, there are still some of the older townspeople who only really feel at home in the church they attended in childhood. Not so long ago I overheard a worshipper say "Well, she's Trinity, she never feels happy in St. Mary's". Of course, this was before St. Mary's was made redundant.

St. Mary's, the parish church, had a curate as well as a Vicar. He was usually a favourite with the children. He was in charge of the Sunday School, organised the sports at the annual outdoor treat, and had not got a wife to tell him it was unbecoming for him to be 'hail fellow and well-met' with the poor of the parish.

St. Mary's church Sunday School was held in the Mission Hall in Broad Street. Infants had the upper floor, and the seniors the big ground floor which had small rooms opening off it for separate classes. The stairs to the upper room were wide and had a banister which was well polished by boys sliding down its slippery length. The winter Sunday School treat was held here too. The lower room was filled with long trestle tables for tea, and the upper one used for party games and sometimes a magic lantern or a conjurer. Sunday School teachers spent the morning getting things ready, cutting bread and butter. There were no conveniently sliced loaves then.

"Put plenty of butter on the bread", said the helpers, "Children can't eat 'bread and scrape' ".

The summer treat was often held on the Big Common, with swings and sports and coconut shies. This was not a very private place, and children from other Sunday Schools would try to gate-crash or merely perch on the fence by the railway line and make mischievous comments on the proceedings.

Occasionally a farmer in the district would lend his meadow for the summer outing and this was a real and much looked forward to treat. Many extra prayers were sent up to Heaven petitioning for a hot sunny day. Perhaps the best part of the outing was the ride from Bungay to the appointed meadow, usually about three miles distant in a wagonette. To children who had to rely on their own strong legs for transport, and who got great enjoyment even from a ride in a wheelbarrow, it was the height of bliss to go jogging along behind a sturdy farm horse, however bone-shaking the wagonette might be.

Tea was delicious eaten in a big lofty barn smelling of hay and turnips and mysteriously hazy when the sun filtered through ages of corn dust. The meadow grass was richer than the dry grass of the Common, and children from rival Sunday Schools were not sitting on a convenient fence to shout out that they could see the mark where your last summer's white dress had been 'let down'; or that you had taken in last year's Sunday hat for 'second best'. Because, of course, all children wore hats even at a picnic and Sunday School treat. Straw hats in summer and felt or velvet hats in winter for the girls. These had elastic under the chin to keep them from blowing off in the wind. The straw hats were pretty, bedecked with satin ribbon or sprays of artificial forget-me-nots, or rosebuds, or even buttercups. Boys had cloth caps in summer and winter, although a few of them with doting mothers were forced to wear straw 'cheese cutter' hats in summer.

The Trinity Church children had their Sunday School in the Trinity Rooms. This was much smaller than St. Mary's Mission Hall, and always smelled of stale gas. There were also the Congregational, Wesleyan, and Primitive Methodist Chapels. The latter, which stood in Laburnum Road, was demolished at the beginning of the Second World War because it was thought to be unsafe. There was a Baptist Chapel in Chaucer Street. The building is still there. I think the attendance was small, but every Sunday a party of worshippers arrived there from the country. A pony trap was driven by a handsome girl with dark hair tied back under a plain straw hat. The other occupants were elderly, indeed one gentleman with a beard seemed to us to be as old as Methuselah, and we felt slightly sorry for the girl who seemed to have no young friends and who had to wear a boy's 'cheese-cutter' hat. The door of this Chapel was always closed so we could never take a peep inside, but it was said that there was a huge tank of water there for Baptisms, and those to be baptised were completely immersed.

Last but by no means least, was the Salvation Army. This was very well attended years ago, and now, like the Primitive Methodists and (until recently) the Baptists, has disappeared from the town.

The Salvation Army gathered around the Town Pump on Saturday evenings and at least twice on Sundays. The lassies in their navy blue bonnets and skirts, which seemed dowdy even in those days of rather plain female attire, waved tambourines and tried to make their thin voices heard above the trumpets and cornets and the beating drum. The Market Place was always crowded with people, especially on Saturday evenings. Shops were kept open for as long as people wanted to go in and buy. Saturday evening was usually the time for family shopping because many employees did not get their wages until work finished on the Saturday. Young men stood on the pavement or leant against the King's Head or Three Tuns walls. The Salvation Army collected its ha'pence in one of the Army helmets, and handed out their weekly journal the 'War Cry'. In all weathers the Army gathered there round the Town Pump, singing often with the added accompaniment of the beating rain and the gurgling of water in the gutters. Raindrops scintillated like diamonds on the gaslit pavements. Joyfully the Army gave voice –

> "When He cometh, when He cometh to take up His Jewels,
> All His Jewels, precious Jewels, His loved and His own".

Then, after more singing and prayers, the Band

and its followers would march slowly from the Market Place back to the Meeting House in Bridge Street.

Occasionally the Salvation Army held its service in other parts of the town, even just outside the gates of St. Mary's church. When the loud crescendo of their band drowned the words of the Vicar's sermon, there would be a stifled giggle among the young people, and angry frowns from the old and staid. But the area around the Town Pump was their customary meeting place. The Town Pump, big and ugly, and always untidy, with spillings of water from the many buckets that were filled there – yet it was solid and loveable, and a real part of the town; and sometimes in the summer, when the puddles had dried for a while, it seemed to rest, dreaming in the sunshine, with the dignity of an aged but much respected part of the community.

The Town Pump indeed, had many uses. Tradesmen's bikes were often propped against it while the errand boys had a quick game of marbles. Bills of forthcoming events were pasted on its sides. But mainly it supplied drinking water to a great number of households, particularly those in the vicinity of the Market Place, and St. Mary's and Earsham Street. Some fortunate people had pumps in their gardens, or there would be one in a backyard to serve a row of cottages. Otherwise, there were tanks and water butts at back doors to catch the rain water for washing purposes, and it would be scooped out into the basin in small galvanised handcups. But this water did not go very far in dry weather, and then it was necessary to join the weary band of men and boys who filled their buckets at the Town Pump. Often they would carry two pails at a time, and plod homewards, jerking out splashes of water with every heavy step. The pump water was sparkling and cold, and very good to drink.

Drinking water for the Printing Works was obtained from the Town Pump. A boy was paid the sum of one shilling and sixpence a week to carry pails of water to a tank which stood in the Printing Works yard. Employees wanting a drink of water would let down a jam jar on a piece of string. In warm weather, the water in the tank became tepid, and often had flies swimming in it.

It was not until 1923 that tap water was available to most dwellings; and even then, the tap was often fixed to a wall in the back yard, as many of the smaller cottages had no kitchen sink. In 1933, the Town Pump was knocked over by a steam wagon. The Town Reeve, Dr. L.B. Cane then considered it to be a public hazard, and ordered it to be demolished, despite some opposition from those who wished to have it preserved. It was replaced by an electric light standard, on which the Black Dog of Bungay snarls defiantly at all who pass by.

Before the Cinema came to Bungay, the building in Broad Street which is now a textile factory, had various uses. Roller-skating was held there. I can remember being dumped on a hard seat and told to be a good girl and watch, while my brother and sister joined in the skating. I can only remember people rushing about on wheels (roller-skates), just managing not to collide with each other, and my legs getting 'pins and needles', because they did not reach the floor. When I arrived home, I told my mother firmly "I am not going anymore to see those clockwork people".

A Bazaar was held there sometimes, and was a happier occasion for young children than the skating. Many cheap but pretty knick-knacks were sold – gay pottery, and little bracelets made of tiny coloured beads. There were imitation watches, and celluloid topsy-turvy men which always landed right side up, however they were placed.

Then the Corn Hall became the Cinema, or Picture Palace. The Saturday afternoon entertainment must have been a great boon to busy mothers, when, for a penny a head, children could be safely entertained for two or three hours while the Saturday afternoon housework was being done. It was a busy time for the housewife, with a great batch of baking to do, and a last minute tidying up, so that as little as possible was left to be done on Sunday – so that it could be the 'Day of Rest' it was intended to be. I think the Commandment that brought most comfort to parents of big families was 'Remember the Sabbath Day to keep it Holy. Six days shalt Thou Labour and do all thy Work, but the Seventh is the Sabbath of the Lord thy God'.

So in our house and in many others there was no sewing, or even knitting and only the minimum of cooking. Story books and comics were thrust away out of sight. Only 'good' books were allowed – 'Audrey or the Children of Light', 'Clara's Confirmation', etc. We all enjoyed reading, and a book was a book, whatever its contents, so we seldom complained that a book was 'dry'. However, I always thought in unfair that my brothers were allowed to read Dickens on Sundays, and my favourite Angela Brazil was forbidden.

Sometimes we sorted our texts of which we had a large collection. They were small cards bearing a design of flowers, birds or trees, and printed with a short text, 'The Lord is Thy Keeper', 'I will not Leave Thee nor forsake Thee'. We were given these by the Sunday School teacher. Mama wrote letters to aunts and cousins. She would ask "Shall I send your love to Aunt Alice?" or to "Cousin Harold". We always said yes, hardly knowing the person in question except that he or she lived at Basingstoke or St. Albans or some other strange place, and sent cards and perhaps presents at Christmas time. To us then, Basingstoke was as far away as New York, or the Cape of Good Hope.

It may sound dull, but we liked our Sundays. They were special days, quite different from weekdays, standing out in the memory as happy times with the parents relaxed from their daily round, and taking us for a delightful afternoon or evening walk. Occasionally we could have a friend to tea. It was always on Sundays we welcomed a friend or went out to tea ourselves.

The pealing of St. Mary's bells, and the ding-dong of Holy Trinity, the trumpets and drums of the Salvation Army Band, all created an exhilarating atmosphere, a kind of exultation which is missing now. Sunday is just another day. Father digs his garden, Mother hangs out the washing, and a line of cars bumper to bonnet take a dusty caterpillar crawl to the seaside.

CHAPTER FOUR

# Town Bells

On Sunday mornings the bells of St. Mary's clashed and clanged and echoed and re-echoed up and down the streets, sending their lovely peal around the town, over the countryside, and away into the distant hills. Softly, but insistently came the single bell of Holy Trinity, and if the wind were westerly, there sounded across the marshes the gentle ding, dong, of All Saints, Earsham; and then the Salvation Army in the Market Place, banging its drum and blowing its trumpet with a music louder than them all.

The pealing of the bells was exciting and exhilarating, to young people at least, and children skipped along the pavements more lightly at the sound of them. Unlike the irritating dong, dong of the school bell on weekdays which made us feel an urge to loiter at the gate for a last game of marbles, and to try to think of a good excuse for being late. The Wingfield Street school, and the Catholic School in St. Mary's Street, each had its summoning bell. The Printing Works also called its workers in the morning and after the lunch hour with five minutes pulling of a ting-tang bell (later replaced by a 'hooter' or siren). The firemen's cart had a magnificent brass bell that boomed like a gong as the Fire Engine, drawn by two galloping horses tore around the street corners, the firemen in their brass helmets looking so different from the everyday Bob or Bill or Fred who delivered our groceries and meat. The gladiators of old could not have been more dashing and exciting to young children.

When there had been a death in the town, the Passing Bell was tolled. A solitary bell from St. Mary's mournfully tolled out the number of years of the dead person's age. An important personage had a muffled bell that gave out such a mournful, stifled sound that you were filled with an unbearable sadness as if your heart-beats were muffled too.

Apart from the Town Crier's bell, and all the various shop door bells, which I have mentioned before, the little white pony that drew the cart of 'Icecream Joe' had bells on its harness. 'Icecream Joe' came only on Sunday afternoons, and only in the hottest weather. The sound of the pony's bells could be heard a street away in the quiet of the Sabbath afternoons, when the church bells had stopped and the members of the Salvation Army were no doubt taking a well-earned rest. The little white pony enjoyed having its neck patted by the children. The cart it drew was very pretty, painted white, with pink roses on the sides.

'Icecream Joe' was an Italian, a dark-haired,

moustachioed man, and his conversation was little more than a nod and a smile; but his ha'penny cornets were most generously filled, and between the penny wafers the icecream was an inch thick. We thought it the most creamy, icy, delicious icecream available. At that time, of course, it had no real competition, because the army of vans that now patrol the roads and streets had not come into existence. The icecream made by Parravani, 'Icecream Joe', had no rival then, and many local people still think it unrivalled in its creamy excellence. For although 'Icecream Joe' and his white pony, with its collar of bells and the pretty painted cart have gone, he left his icecream recipe behind, and his family continue to make it for new generations to enjoy.

On Sundays, when the church bells rang out, all the places of worship were well attended, and after the services, many people would take a walk, if the weather was good, to help them digest the sermon, and to give them an appetite for their midday meal. The favourite walk was along Earsham Dam, empty of traffic, and with the pleasant sound of the water at 'Roaring Arch' rippling over the stones. Why we called such a tiny eddy the 'Roaring Arch', I do not know, but throwing a twig into the water and watching it rush through the arch, tossed and churned in the white frothing whirlpool gave a breathless moment of excitement and fear that pictures of the Niagara Falls could never invoke.

We would leave the main road and walk along the Wolds by the riverside to look with longing eyes at the forget-me-nots and red ragged-robins which we were not allowed to pick on Sundays. The reason for this was not religious, but economic; our parents feared we would slip at the water's edge and spoil our best Sunday clothes. However, Dadda might oblige by reaching a yellow flag iris with his walking stick, or hook a red ragged-robin nearer the bank towards us. The river, although part of the Waveney, was very narrow, and usually so much covered with bright green duckweed, dotted with white water buttercups that very little of the water could be seen.

Most men carried walking sticks on Sundays, and Mama had an umbrella, or sunshade, and always wore a veil. How enviously I used to watch my mother manipulate her veil (usually of black net), smooth it under her chin, and tie it somehow or other behind her neck. Veils have now gone out of fashion, except for the silly little bits of net that dangle over one eye in some millinery concoctions.

So also have disappeared the black velvet chokers with clusters of brilliants, and the really lethal looking long spiked hat-pins. My mother had a large assortment of these which I was forbidden to touch.

My memories of the 'Roaring Arch' are not altogether happy. On a sunny morning during the school summer holiday, I was playing with some friends by the water there. It was not very deep, but it flowed swiftly through the arch, and then dropped a few inches into the river, churning the water into a small whirlpool, white crested and eddying. We always found it fascinating as we sat on the bank to watch.

"It's not very deep", I said. One of my friends retorted, "I bet you daren't paddle right in it!"

Who could resist a dare? I slid down the bank, and dabbled my foot in the swirling water. Before I had got very far, my friends rushed off home, and kindly informed my mother. "Please, Mrs. Ottaway, Iris is paddling in the Roaring Arch!"

I was met by a very angry parent; and I resented the fact that she had listened to my friends' story, without hearing my excuses. "You could have been drowned", my mother cried. "Well", I replied, with uncharacteristic pertness, "It was me being drowned, not you!"

"No back answers", said my mother. "You will spend the whole afternoon shut in the sitting-room".

"Please don't lock the door", I cried. I have always had a horror of being locked in. "And may I have a book?"

"No, you may not have a book". After she had gone, I looked round my prison. Staring at me from the wall was a large copy of a painting of Lord Roberts, the military hero, a favourite of my mother's. I hated it! The colours of his regimental dress were too bright, and I had never liked red. His eyes, blue and hard seemed to follow me round the room. I felt that I must do something to get away from their cold accusation. I looked at the bookcases. Grown-up books, but I could read anything. I noticed a very large volume of 'Prayers and Devotions'. It was one that my grandfather used to read aloud before breakfast. Surely I could be allowed to look through that. I reached the heavy book down, and opened it at random.

"You who are not of the Catholic Faith", it stated, then something about not being fit to enter the Kingdom of Heaven. I broke out in a cold sweat. I was not a Catholic. We were members of St. Mary's church, although I attended the Catholic school because it was considered to provide a better education than the school in Wingfield Street. The headmistress there was fond of describing the horrors of hell. Protestants had no chance. The best they could hope for was Purgatory. That sounded to me like sitting on a dark cold stairway between Heaven and Hell.

If I had told my mother, she would have explained the difference to me between the Catholic faith and Roman Catholicism. Instead, I held the worry close to me, and for a long time afterwards I lay awake at night, drenched in perspiration at the thought of the horrors of hell-fire.

## CHAPTER FIVE

# Public Houses

If the churches were well attended, so also were the pubs, and these were much more numerous than they are today. On the outskirts of the town where Flixton Road meets the crossroads at the foot of St. Margaret's Hill stood the 'Thatched House'. This was small and looked like a cottage with an untidy front yard, usually occupied by a tumbril or a horse standing patiently by a governess cart. This was a very isolated building and must have been dreary indeed on a winter's night. Behind it was the narrow winding road that led to St. Margaret's, bordered on one side with ploughland, and on the other with a lonely plantation of fir trees. From the 'Thatched House' to what is now the Flixton Road Post Office, about a quarter of a mile away there was no other dwelling at all. The road was lined with oak trees which almost met overhead and made a beautiful leafy tunnel delightful to walk under in summer, but quite frightening on a winter's night when gales lashed the trees and tore at the tormented branches.

Indeed, the 'Thatched House' was pleasant enough in summer with birds calling in the nearby copse all day, and the nightingale singing there at night. At that time, when nobody hit the headlines for walking twenty five miles for charity, the walk called the 'Homersfield Round' was a pleasant Sunday afternoon or evening stroll. From Bungay the walkers would go along Earsham Dam and Temple Bar to Earsham 'Buck' and then on to Homersfield 'Swan'. Then along the Flixton Hall road, where bracken grew close to the track and rabbits would scuttle across the path. In the Hall grounds, a deer might lift its head suddenly and startled by the sight of humans, dash away to cover. Flixton 'Buck' faced the Hall gates, and from the Buck to the 'Thatched House' was almost three miles of tree-lined road, with one or two farmhouses as the only mark of civilisation. Otherwise, there were trees and high grassy banks, and ditches full of dead leaves or water or primroses according to the season. This walk was not what is vulgarly called a 'pub crawl', but a pleasant means of exercise by people young and middle aged, who enjoyed each other's company; and a call at the inn for a glass of ale or ginger beer and a few words with the inn-keeper and his good lady gave extra enjoyment to the evening's outing.

On Market Day, too, the 'Thatched House' would be busy with country people taking refreshment before climbing the long hill to Three Ashes. Thursday was Market Day, and whatever the weather, the town was crowded with farmers and other country folk from the Parishes and Earsham and Ditchingham. On the pavement outside the 'King's Head', farming folk congregated, cloth-capped and red-faced, talking of farm prices and stock prices and the terrible state of the country; but not looking at all anxious about the outcome of these affairs.

There were always dogs wandering disconsolately, looking for their masters, but by the end of the afternoon the dogs would be trotting happily homeward behind their masters' carts, or seated proudly in the front seat between the farmer and his lady. And that surely is the best way to travel home. Behind a leisurely trotting horse, the reins held loosely along its swaying back, the purring of the cart wheels and time to really see the trees and hedges with their infinite variety of colour and bud, changing week by week and season by season. Time to look across the undulating Suffolk fields, newly ploughed, brown or green, with winter wheat, or ripening gold to harvest, right away to the blue horizon. Time to point one's whip and make the oft repeated comments, warm in their very familiarity:–

"Funny how that old tree got struck by lightning".

"That corn's coming along a treat. There'll be a good harvest, God willing".

"About time old Ben got that fence mended";

And so the end of another Market Day, a natter with friends, a grumble about the government, a drink or two, and so home to the satisfying country life of the farmer.

About a quarter of a mile from the 'Thatched House' into Bungay stands the 'Oak' in Bardolph Road. The tree from which it got its name is no longer there, but it was a magnificent tree standing in a small garden in front of the inn. Now the garden and tree are gone to make way for a parking space for cars. The opposite side of the road, Honeypot Meadow had its trees too. There was a steep grassy bank and a high hedge bordering the meadow. At the top of the bank was a small patch, almost an elfin track made by the feet of children, for it was their delight to run to the top of the bank and look down on their elders walking on the road below. The trees were mainly oaks, but there was also an ash which was no doubt watched anxiously in spring. If it came into leaf before the oak, there would be a very wet summer:

'Oak before ash, there'll be a splash;
Ash before oak, we're in for a soak'.

The bowling green stands nearby, so the oak coming into leaf early seemed to promise long bright summer evenings of sending the ball smoothly along the velvet grass and hearing it reach its mark with a satisfying thud.

Part of the Honeypot Meadow was a recreation ground. The town Football Club played there and spectators stood two deep outside on the road or in a bordering lane, called the Folly, to get a free view of the match over the low hedge. Sports were held there, too, and it was the rallying ground for marches or carnival processions before they paraded round the town. Honeypot Meadow, was, in a small way, the Common of the South end of the town, and children played there under the oak trees. At one time it was suggested as a good site for a swimming pool, something which has always been needed in the island town of Bungay, with the surrounding Waveney a danger to non-swimmers. Now, of course a swimming pool has eventually been built, but not in the town centre as originally planned.

The trees are all gone now, and in their place is a well laid out estate of houses for the elderly, somewhat inappropriately called the 'Honeypot'. At one point in the bank there used to be some worn steps leading to a break in the hedge with a gate leading to a large chicken run. Often on a winter's afternoon I have seen a very old man climb those steps with a bucket of food for the hens. Silently he plodded up the broken steps and pushed open a low wooden gate. Having fed his fowls, he walked slowly back down the steps again, looking neither to right, nor to left, speaking to no-one, not even to his chickens.

Almost every back garden had its dozen or so hens, with an arrogant glossy-necked cockerel strutting among them. In the Spring, coops would appear on a patch of grass and then a wire-netting covered run, housing the newly hatched fluffy yellow and black chicks with their incredibly soft heads and bright beady eyes. One misses the crowing of cocks to herald the start of a new day, the cackling of hens in mid-morning, and that strange soft clucking made by hens and cockerels alike as they peck and scratch contentedly and freely in the yards.

From Flixton Road along Upper Olland Street and into St. Mary's Street were the 'Rose & Crown', the 'Greyhound', the 'Anchor' and the 'Prince of Wales', the 'Fleece', the 'Swan' and the 'Bell' and in the parallel Lower Olland Street, the 'Angel' and the 'Ship'. In the Market Place itself are the 'King's Head', and the 'Three Tuns', and at the top of Bridge Street was the 'Queen'. In Cross Street stood the 'Crown'. The 'Two Brewers' was in Chaucer Street, and the 'Horse and Groom' in Broad Street; in Earsham Street the 'White Lion'. Almost as far as the Common was the 'Cherry Tree'; and on the bridge just into Norfolk at Ditchingham was the 'Falcon'.

For a population of around three thousand, the drinking public was well catered for. In all there were thirty-three public houses.

Adjoining most of the 'pubs' were double wooden gates with the words 'Good Stabling' painted on them. These gates were often swinging open, and on windy days creaked in chorus with the swaying Inn signs above them.

None of them had very original names, although 'The Ship' and 'The Angel' are the most inappropriate. The 'Falcon' by the Waveney, and the 'White Horse' also by the river near the Staithe seemed the most imaginative and romantic. Both pubs must have been very busy in the days when Wherries came up the river from

Beccles as far as Bungay.

Now of the thirty-three pubs which existed in my youth, very few are left. Some have been converted to shops, for example, 'The Bell', which is now a relevision and radio shop. Some have been converted to dwelling houses; and the size of the yard behind, and the large sheds and outbuildings still standing, show that there was room at the Inn for a few wayfarers, and a warm stable for their horses.

In my childhood I was rather fearful of passing a public house. Many of the books children read at that time, especially those given as Sunday School prizes, were often unhappy stories of young children hungry and ragged because the breadwinner "drank all his money away". Of course, the stories usually ended happily, with the drunkard seeing the error of his ways, and becoming a model parent. 'Audrey or the Children of Light', and 'Clara's Confirmation' were two stories of this type, which were old favourites.

The Sunday School also organised a gathering called 'The Band of Hope'. My elder sister and brothers attended this, and used to talk mysteriously of "signing the pledge"; and sang gay little ditties, such as

"My drink is Water bright, Water bright,
From the crystal stream".

I was intrigued by these mysteries, and looked forward to joining the 'Band of Hope', and "signing the pledge" when I was old enough, but the meetings must have been discontinued, for I never attended one.

There was usually a loud, but somewhat warm and companionable hum of conversation coming from the public houses I passed, rising and falling but never reaching the height of anger. There was always, too, the sound of someone playing a tinny piano, thumping out the tunes of the day. Sometimes a sudden loud guffaw of laughter would cause me to look back fearfully, and then, with a toss of the head, I ran like mad until I reached the safety of our own garden gate.

## CHAPTER SIX

# Strange Characters

There were many odd characters in the town. Some we loved, of others we were frankly terrified. I wonder where all such odd folk are now? Perhaps we are all now so odd that the eccentric is no longer noticed. When mini-skirts and midi-skirts and maxi-skirts walk side by side, and fat legs bulge over high white boots, and labourers have hair flowing from an 'Alice band' down to their waists, and wear bead necklaces, there is little left to cause eyebrows to lift in surprise.

Elderly ladies walk about hatless in pretty flowered dresses, and, seen from behind, could be any age. Years ago a person's age, particularly a woman's, could be judged by the dress she wore. When girls left school, they turned up their long hair into a bun, and wore ankle-length skirts. Married women had even longer skirts, and very sober coloured clothes, dark grey or navy or brown. At sixty, women were really old, and wore little black bonnets and black capes. Small boys had long dresses until they reached the age of three. I remember just before the First World War, my younger brother getting his first knickerbocker suit and discarding his long serge dress with its white sailor collar. It was quite an event in his young life and for the rest of the family who stood round admiring him.

One of the most loveable of our characters was an elderly gentleman known as Little Jimmy. He was small, of frail build, and shorter than most fourteen year old boys. He always wore a long shabby tweed coat, which probably made him seem even shorter, and a large cloth cap. He moved along with jerky little running steps, as if he was always in a hurry, and he carried always a shiny black shopping bag.

The shopping bag alone would have made him conspicuous, because at that time, men did not do the shopping. That was a task for women and children, and if a man ever did shop, his purchases would be stuffed in his pocket out of sight. But Jimmy kept house for a scholarly brother and did the housework and cooking as well as the shopping. The brother was in direct contrast; immaculately dressed in a black suit, and hard black trilby hat, and a shining gold watch across his chest. One would never have dared say "Good morning" as he paced along slowly, hands behind his back, eyes looking at the ground. But everybody said good-day to his brother; and Jimmy would pause in his hurried walk and smile and begin to say "G g g g ood morning"; for unfortunately he stammered. And if any unkind child teased or mimicked him, the smile would fade from his wrinkled face. He would shake his head sadly, or even lift his walking stick threateningly before he continued on his busy way.

Down 'Borough Well' steps lived Maggie Murphy – at least she was rumoured to live there, although I do not know of anybody who actually saw her. On darkening winter evenings, children would go tip-toeing by the opening of the steps; and, if any child said – "Look! There's Old Maggie Murphy", there would be a mad rush of all the children towards the welcome glow of a lighted shop window.

Another elderly lady, known as 'Bun Annie' pushed a covered barrow up the steep Bridge Street, and along Trinity Street and Staithe Road. A delicious smell of new bread and brandy snaps and spicy currant buns came from the barrow. In all weathers Bun Annie wore a long wide skirted dress and a dilapidated straw hat. They were no doubt black originally, but had become, with age, the colour of rust. Children trotted alongside, offering to "have a go" at pushing the barrow. Annie took no heed of them and trudged steadily on her way, eyes downcast and her hands clenched so tightly over the wooden handles that the barrow seemed to be part of her. Wisps of black hair strayed from her bonnet but one saw little of her downcast face.

There was a very evangelical looking gentleman who lived with his wife in one of the Almshouses on the Drift (Outney Road). On Sundays and weekdays alike he was dressed in black. His frock coat had an old-fashioned cut even at that time, and his wide brimmed black felt hat topped a round benignly smiling pink face. His beard was snow white and long, almost to his waist. He liked to meet the children from school, and he gave them sweets and patted their heads and asked what they had learned that day. He seemed to be altogether good and holy like an imaginary Abraham straight from the Bible; but it was said that he was really a man with a wicked temper, who made his wife wait on him hand and foot. He insisted on having his morning cocoa made with the water from his hot-water bottle.

Hot-water bottles were not so common then, and the rubber or 'jelly-bottles', as they were first called, were unheard of. The old earthenware bottles were weighty and unwieldy to lift, but they kept very hot. Some people used to heat flat-irons in winter. They were wrapped in thick flannel and placed at the foot of the bed.

Anyhow, this old gentleman became more and more bad-tempered and eccentric, and eventually had to be 'put away'. This was a polite way of saying that he had gone to the 'Sylum, another mysterious place.

We were a healthy community and it was unusual to see a lame or sickly child, but there was a 'dwarf' in the town. She was probably in her mid-twenties when we knew her, but to children anybody over school age was 'old' especially at that time when young people went into grown up clothes so soon. She seemed old to us, although she was about as tall as a sturdy three-year-old; but she was as broad as she was long, and her long black dress and large black straw hat from which two long pigtails hung almost to the ground, and her ambling gait gave her an unwieldy look. Children teased her, but she spoke to nobody. Sometimes she would stand stockstill and stare at them silently. There was a sort of dignity in the strangely shaped creature that must have shamed those who taunted her; for they would soon stop their teasing, and slink silently away.

I must mention 'Blind Joe', who stood at the 'kissing-gate' which led on to the Big Common from the railway bridge. He was always there on fine Sunday afternoons, and on special occasions such as Race Meetings, Fairs, or cricket matches, when a steady flow of people might be expected on the Common. He had round his neck a card-board placard on which was printed 'Please Help the Poor Blind Bungay Man'. He held out a hard black bowler hat to take offerings. Sometimes his wife would be with him playing on a 'to-and-from' (accordion).

Many of the townspeople entering the gate would say "Afternoon, Joe", or "Hello, Joe", and he often replied, "Afternoon, George", or "Hello, Mrs. Bailey". I asked my mother how could Blind Joe know the names of the people who spoke to him if he were really blind? She replied that he had been in the town so long that he had got to recognise people's voices. I puzzled over this, and thought perhaps he could open his eyes a little and so recognise some people.

He and his wife also stood outside the gates of the Printing Works on Friday evenings when the men left off work. There were other beggars waiting there too, hoping for a generous copper from some of the 'printers' on Friday, Pay Night.

I cannot put Blind Joe into the category of beggar. In his rusty black suit and his bowler hat, he had a certain dignity, and would hold back the heavy gate with an old world air of courtesy. His wife, by contrast, looked shoddy in a full-length coat, very old and threadbare, that swept the ground as she walked.

But my favourite 'people' were not alive at all. In the large shop window of Mr. Rowe, the men's outfitter's, stood two wax models of young boys in tweed suits, with hard round collars. The younger one wore what was called a knickerbocker suit. His face was so beautiful with the pink and white wax complexion. His thick-lashed eyes were piercing blue, his hair thick and curly. The older boy wore a Norfolk jacket, but I hardly looked at him. My eyes were on the handsome younger one, who looked straight back at me – my first love! As I attended the Catholic School in St. Mary's Street, I had the opportunity of seeing my favourite model very often.

CHAPTER SEVEN

# The Picture Palace

On Saturday afternoons, children came from every street in the town, clutching their pennies in sticky hands, and skipping and hopping or running on their eager way to the "Pictures". The 'Picture House' was the old Fisher Theatre at the Market end of Broad Street, not the Mayfair Cinema which was not built until the 1930s. The door was never opened until just before the performance was due to start, so the crowd gathered outside, chattering and sucking noisily on their hard-boiled sweets. It was quite safe for them to spread themselves across the road, at this top end of Broad Street. The Station Goods yard at the Common end was closed on Saturday afternoons, so the street was empty of the horse drawn carts and wagons that usually rumbled slowly up and down.

The Cinema performance was probably not very good entertainment and was certainly not educational, but it "moved", and much of it was exciting, and the piano accompaniment seemed more exhilarating than the electric organ which later superceded it. A pianist played throughout the whole programme, and how her fingers must have ached as they sped along in time to the galloping horses hooves, and how the childrens' feet pounded on the floor in accord, and how all the little hearts raced as the horses rushed to seeming destruction and then reared back from the edge of a cliff top, held in the superhuman grip of the hero. How the racing music reached a crescendo, and then stopped with a great crashing of chords as the screen turned white, and the black lettering asked all who could read, "Will the Red Ace escape? What has happened to Marian? See next week's thrilling episode – Part 6, The Red Ace Meets His Doom!" All children who could read, read this aloud, which of course was a great help to the younger ones. The serial was always the climax of the performance, and the magnet that drew an audience week after week, until that particular story was finished.

Bill posters stuck vividly coloured bills on various walls in the town on Monday mornings, advertising the following Saturday's performance. At twelve o'clock on Monday there was a rush from school to the first hoarding which displayed the deadly perils that awaited the hero and heroine. More than life-size pictures of real he-men, with stubborn jaws and cowboy hats pushed to the back of scrubbing brush hair. Beautiful girls with their blue eyes round with terror, and their tiny red buttoned-up mouths pouting. The supporting programme usually consisted of short comic items – custard pies being thrown indiscriminately, and old men falling with a crash (accompanied by piano chords) on a greasy floor. This broad humour delighted the children and many of the boys imitated the somersaulting and falling down on their way home.

Short episodes of Charlie Chaplin were shown at that time, and later on, Jackie Coogan. These were great favourites, although some viewers could have found Charlie Chaplin a sad character to be wept over rather than laughed at. His dark mournful eyes as he hung around cafes hoping for a stray bun, his toes sticking out of holey socks and holier boots, as he stood out in the rain, water dripping from his shabby old bowler hat. Even the ridiculous little walking stick he twiddled incessantly seemed a dejected thing, and the whole character cried out for pity.

Later came the cartoons of 'Felix the Cat'. Felix became a household word, and the song "Felix Kept on Walking" was sung ad nauseum. Felix, the wonder cat, who survived countless adventures, and although blown up with dynamite and suffering innumerable other deaths and disasters, "kept on walking still".

Sometimes the Cinema was hired for the annual winter treat of the Sunday Schools. Tea was served in the respective school halls, and then all denominations, walking in crocodile fashion, congregated at the "Pictures". Walking through the dark streets on a winter's evening was thrilling in itself to children who were not allowed by their parents to play outside after dark. The Cinema seemed to be brilliantly lit in comparison with the dark streets outside, and there was much owlish blinking of eyes and excited chattering.

"What are we going to see?" (The Picture to be shown was always a well-kept secret).

"Cinderella?"

"No, we saw that last year".

"I wouldn't mind seeing that again. Cor, them ugly ole sisters. Talk about laughing! They made me die, they did!"

"Well, you aren't dead, are you".

Then the lights would fade, and the hall filled with an eerie gloom, smelling of stale tobacco smoke, and stale gas. Then an arc of dusty light came from the magic box at the back of the hall, and the empty white screen stood out in the darkness. The exciting letters appeared: 'JACK AND THE BEANSTALK'.

All the children took in a deep breath, which they seemed to hold, spellbound, while Jack and his cow confronted the Giant, and finally outwitted him. The Picture was always flickering, often hazy, sometimes it 'broke'. Then there were agonised moments of suspense. The lights went up, and friends stared strangely at each other as if they had been jolted too suddenly from the Story Book Land to plain reality. The 'break' was usually quickly repaired before the children got too impatient; and the Giant continued with his Fee-Fo-Fumming, as if nothing had happened. The treat did not end there, for as the children filed out from the hall, each was given a gaily painted box full of sweets, an orange, and two bright newly minted ha'pennies.

## CHAPTER EIGHT

# The River

The River Waveney, which takes a horseshoe bend around Bungay, is at its widest by the Falcon public house. On the side of the river opposite the Falcon was the somewhat ambitiously named Boat Yard. In fact, there were half a dozen or so rowing boats moored by the river side. There was a great demand for the hire of these, at sixpence an hour, especially on summer evenings, Sunday afternoons and Bank Holidays. Indeed, it was well to order in advance to avoid disappointment.

The river also winds in a great curve around the Common, and is not wide at any point. Many inexperienced rowers could spend an hilarious hour colliding with the banks in a slow and zigzag progress. The banks were gay with wild flowers in the summer, especially with water forget-me-nots, unrivalled in their deep blue by any grown in gardens; also the purple river mint, water buttercups, and the big yellow water-lilies on their islands of leaves with their cloying vanilla scent.

Rowing towards the Common, the boats would pass under the railway bridge, which carried the Harleston to Beccles line. What excitement to be passing under the bridge when a train was speeding overhead! Then onwards over the water to the low rickety footbridge, halfway round the Common with cries of "Duck your head!"; and along to Bath Hills, a wooded slope which from the river, seemed to tower up to the sky. On one side the pine-scented woods, and on the other, the green stretch of Common, in the summer filled with grazing cattle and horses, and the panoramic view of the town with the tall grey church tower standing sentinel over the cluster of houses, seeming so remote. No streets, no shops, no gardens in the intervening distance, it appeared alone uninhabited and quite mysterious.

It was on the Common that the Race Meetings were held. There were two events each year, one in April and the other in September. The April event was a two-day meeting, on Wednesday and Thursday, and was an important occasion to which children and adults alike looked forward with eagerness. School children had two half-days off. Wednesday was "early closing", so shop owners and their assistants were free. The Printing Works gave employees Thursday afternoon off, so there was a great hurrying of feet towards the Common on both days. Visitors came from all over East Anglia, and even further afield. It was an occasion for inviting friends and relatives to stay, and of suddenly running into an acquaintance one had not seen since last race day. There were extra trains from Yarmouth and Norwich because at that time there was no bus service and very few people owned cars. Many came in by pony cart or a Brake that carried about a dozen passengers in its precarious looking swaying top.

For many, especially the children, the thrill of the Races started on the Tuesday evening when a special train brought the race-horses in big van-like horse boxes. Crowds gathered on the bridge overlooking the railway line long before the train was due, and there was much peering up and down the line for the first puff of smoke to appear above the tree-tops. Then a cry "Here she comes!" and the crowd gazing at the up-line surged to the other side of the bridge, getting well-blackened faces as a cloud of smoke belched out from the train as it slowed down. The brick wall of the railway bridge was too high for smaller children to see over, and there were impatient cries of "Dadda, lift me up! I want to see the horses".

When the train stopped, the sides of the horse-boxes were unfastened, and the horses were led out by jockeys and trainers, and local men who were providing them with stable room. Every available stable was hired out. There were many stables which have now disappeared from the town, and one has hardly noticed their passing. I remember spelling out in my early reading days, the words 'Good Stabling', on so many wooden gates, especially those belonging to public houses. They were usually double doors, and often one half would be shut at 'Good', and the 'Stabling' half would be swinging creakily to and fro. So the horses would be led to these stables, and given a good meal and drink and then bedded down for the night. And what a thrill if you had a friend with a stable so you could steal a peep over the half-door, or even be allowed to stroke one of the horses.

"What is his name? Do you think he's going to win? Sure and Sp'dar. That's a winner alright!"

It was always rumoured that a celebrated jockey, such as Steve Donoghue would be coming to the Races that year, and this heightened the anticipation.

Very early the next morning the town would be woken by the sound of the horses' hooves clopping on the hard roads as they were taken to the Common for a gallop.

The midday meal was put forward that day, and harassed mothers must have found the occasion a mixed blessing, longing to see the first race themselves, and having to get their flock ready with well scrubbed faces and clean clothes, and making sure that Father had put on his clean shirt, "for you never know who you might run into on the Race Course, and I'm not having any of you shame me!"

For these two days, our Common became an unfamiliar place. In addition to the mass of people surging to and fro, with somebody always trying to elbow through the crowd looking for somebody or something, there were also rows of rather ricketty looking stalls, selling sweets, fruits, and even fish. There were slimy looking oysters in little white saucers, and a sudden whiff of vinegar blown on the breeze would make your stomach heave. There were the stands of the bookies. "Place your bet with Honest Joe"; and a great shouting would begin, of "Tiddy one, Bar one". At least that was what I thought the words were until my brother somewhat scathingly corrected me. "It's Two to One, Bar One!"

Then another cry would break out of "Clear the course, clear the course", and a very tall steward would ride down the 'straight' on his beautiful horse, and the people who had been walking along its smooth width to look at the jumps would hurriedly move to either side behind the rails, to await the next race.

There was also, of course, the Grandstand. This seemed an enormous edifice to a child, and it was quite an effort to clamber up all the steps to the top seats, from which there was a magnificent view across the Common. However, there were many pieces of rising ground from which one could get a good view without paying the Grandstand prices; and different race-goers had their favourite vantage points, usually near the start, or finish or close to one of the jumps. The water-jump was a favourite place as there was always the possibility of a horse throwing its rider into the water.

It was delightful to see the jockeys in their gaily coloured blouses and bright caps bobbing up and down in the distance, and to hear the thud of the horses' hooves on the turf, gradually getting nearer and louder. Occasionally a horse fell, and how the crowd would hurry towards the unfortunate spot. Sometimes a horse that had thrown its rider would tear away over the Common. On one occasion a riderless horse swam across the river and somehow made its way on to the Norwich road, where it was eventually caught.

I do not remember hearing of any great misfortunes to horses or jockeys, although sometimes we might overhear our elders speaking of a broken collarbone or concussion. At the time when the Suffragette movement was loudly protesting about the rights of women to gain the vote, it was rumoured that they would come to Bungay Races and blow up the Grandstand. I had visions, especially on dark nights, when the wind was roaring down the chimney, of some enormous masculine looking women standing on the Common in front of the Grandstand, hands on hips, puffing away with all their breath until the Grandstand finally quivered and fell.

On the Thursday evening, the Races would be over, except for the hard luck stories of the winnings that were lost, the horse that should have won, or Honest Joe, who had run off with all his clients' money. For a few days the grass of the Common would be brown and flattened, with untidy rings where stalls had stood, and the ground would be littered with bits of torn up tickets, and coloured betting slips; while the 'tidying-up men' with their spiked sticks would prod around carefully hoping to pick up a fallen banknote.

The trampled buttercups and red sorrel would lift their heads again, and the grass become green. The frightened linnets would fly back to sing in the gorse bushes. The litter of 'pop' bottles would disappear, and the town had time to breathe peacefully until the next exciting occasion of the annual calendar – Bungay May Fair.

A "Pleasure Fair" always came with the Race Meeting. It was so called to distinguish it from Bungay May Fair, a centuries old traditional event for the buying and selling of horses and cattle. This was held on what is known as Fairstead Meadow in St. John's Road. There was plenty of space here for small ponies to wander and crop the Spring grass. A small pony could be bought for as little as thirty shillings, an enviable comparison with the five or six hundred pounds which would be expected today.

Swings and roundabouts and the usual hoop-la and sweet rock stalls and coconut shies were set up here, too. Gradually over the years the trading became less, and now there is no longer a trading fair. The Pleasure Fair has dwindled to a few amusements for children, or stalls where adults can try their luck at winning large fluffy toys. The old Pleasure Fair was held on the Little Common, while the Race Meeting took over the Big Common. The Little Common is now taken over by the Printing Works, but at one time it was an ideal place for small children to play. Mothers could sit and gossip, and do their knitting, and would occasionally rummage in a big shopping bag when one of their offspring ran up to ask for "something to eat". The air of the Common is wonderful for giving folks an appetite.

In summer the grass grew head high, and among the grasses was a profusion of wild flowers, marguerite daisies, purple vetch, cuckoo flowers and ragwort. The hedges abounded with lovely pink delicately scented wild roses. The strong iron railings that fenced the Common from the road were ideal for "topples" and gymnastic feats in an age when none of the local schools had a gymnasium. There was also a sandpit and a short steep slope that led down to the fence enclosing the Station Goods Yard, which made an excellent place for sliding down on old tin trays borrowed from home.

Between the Little Common and the Goods Station was a grass covered lane called a 'loke' down which pigs and young cattle were driven to be loaded on to the cattle train. The pigs arrived from neighbouring farms in a tumbril covered with thick netting, and it was a task indeed for the men to get the pigs out and drive them down the loke to the awaiting truck. They were silly things, squealing piercingly and darting to right and left, but never it seemed, running in front where they were intended to go. On Saturday afternoons the railings that bordered the Station were as full of chattering children as the overhead wires were full of chattering sparrows, all the children having come along to watch the trucks being shunted from line to line.

But during the week that included the two day Race Meeting, the Little Common was taken over by the Pleasure Fair. At the top end were the swings and roundabouts, the stalls and gypsy caravans. The caravans were of course, horse-drawn with half doors opening onto a flight of steps; and their curved roofs had little tiny chimneys always emitting a trail of smoke. Usually a dog was tethered to the caravan and lay underneath and dark-eyed children played round about. On the lower part of the Common the ponies that pulled the caravans had good grazing on the young grass.

Amusements at the Fair would seem very tame to children today, but to us they were exciting and rather breathtaking. It seemed quite daring to ride on the small roundabout with its gaudily painted horses. It was hand propelled by a big wheel and moved only at a snail's pace, compared with the giant racers on pleasure grounds now. We thought it was wonderful to travel around in a small circle and see our parents standing motionless at the place from which we started, and to come round again and again until the music stopped, and the ride finished, and the man at the wheel stood up to stretch his aching back, and we were lifted down by Dadda on to the ground, which seemed to rock unsteadily beneath our feet for several minutes.

"May I go on the big horses next time?" small children would ask, half hoping for a refusal as they watched the second roundabout with its huge shining yellow horses swaying up and down to the strident music and seeming to gallop at a terrible pace as it gathered momentum. This was steam driven, and every now and then 'let off steam' with a terrifying shriek and a shower of spray. The third roundabout was the most wonderful of all, and consisted of ostentatious looking red plush gondola-like seats that raced shudderingly up and down and round and round. From the highest point, probably about eight feet from the ground you had a fleeting glimpse across the great expanse of Common to the trees of Bath Hills, before you were swept down again, and half way up the next slope.

The smell of steam and also of hot rock from the stalls, as well as oysters and crabs from the fish stalls, together with the rattling motion of the roundabout made you feel slightly sick, and so you were quite glad, when the parents said "No more today, it's getting late, you can go on the swing boats tomorrow perhaps". But we always stopped to watch Dadda knock down a coconut, and to buy some of the dark brown streaked peppermint rock to take home. Dragging a little heavily on Dadda's hand, we would leave behind the noisy fairground, with its haunting plaintive mechanical music, which followed us home and lingered into our dreams.

There were race days when a biting wind swept across the Common and hail stung your face, and the horses were hidden from sight by a blur of driving rain that sent people scurrying for shelter. Probably the April races had the usual mixture of sunshine and showers; but I remember mainly the fine days when the sun was warm on our backs and we could sit on the dry grass and drink cold ginger pop without shivering.

May 14th, the date of Bungay May Fair was notorious for its bad weather. "Bungay May Fair Weather" meant anything from cold winds and lowering clouds, to sleety showers, or a real downpour which lasted the entire day. This did not worry us much, for the Fair was not a social occasion like the Races, and the people who gathered there were mainly horse dealers and farmers until the evening, when the young men would take their sweethearts for a ride on the roundabouts, or attempt to win for them one of the cheap, gaudily coloured 'china' ornaments. It was not a popular place for mothers to take young children, for space was congested, and the crowds pushed and elbowed, and there were frequent orders to "Hold tight to my hand", and "All those rough dealers about! You never know!" Why a race-going crowd should be safer and more respectable than the dealers at the May Fair is just one of those prejudices that stick in rural minds. But we liked to be taken along the road to the Wooden Bridge which ran beside the Fair Meadow, and to peep through the hedge to see the little ponies that galloped about the grass until they went up for sale. Sometimes a pony would come close to the hedge to have its soft nose stroked, just as the race horses did from their stable doors.

The area called the Wooden Bridge was delightful to children, for except in a very dry season there was always a trickle of water across the road, running from a dyke beside the Fair

Meadow. After heavy rain, and always during the winter, the trickle became a small river, stretching deep over the road as much as ten yards each side of the bridge. This area has now been drained, and a housing estate is built there. The little bit of stream that is left, children now call the Tin River. We knew the area as Joyce Meadows, one of the most pleasant walks in Bungay; a town surrounded by pleasant walks. Here could be found the earliest primroses and violets in Spring, and a narrow lane led between high banks that blossomed with every kind of wild flower in summer, bright purple vetch, yellow ragwort, orange and yellow bunny-nose, harebells, and marguerite daisies, and the heavenly blue speedwells. The lane led to a wide meadow of rich grass and shady oak trees, and eventually to Shoe-Devil Lane. This was a wide grassy track, famous for blackberries in the autumn, and stretched between the road leading to St. John's, and the narrow road leading to Mettingham Castle.

After the May Fair came the Whitsun Bank Holiday. The big event of Whit Monday was a Sports Meeting held on the Maltings Meadow. In our family it was always a toss-up between going to the sports events, or hiring a rowing boat and taking a picnic tea on the river. Usually the river won, and the sound of the brass band from the Sports meadow could be heard across the Dam while we boated along the water. This delighted my mother, for she loved the music of a brass band.

However, when the boys were older, and very keen on competing in the mile race, and the cycling races, we had to forsake the river and attend the sports meeting to cheer them on. I am sure I was not the only small child who followed the family party with a scowling face, and dragging feet, "kicking up the dust", and muttering bitterly "It's much better on the river, there's nothing to see here".

Sports meetings can be boring for younger children, with grownups pressed against the rails and blocking their view, and having to squint at the proceedings through a sea of legs. The only relief from boredom was Icecream Joe, who was kept busy all the afternoon, dabbing icecream into cornets and wafers.

CHAPTER NINE

# The Railway Station

In this short account of the Bungay beloved of my young days, I must make special mention of the Railway Station. The line ran from Harleston to Beccles, and passing through Bungay, divided the Little Common and the Big Common.

I have mentioned before the enjoyment gained from watching the trains go by, and the shunting of trucks on long, lazy, Saturday afternoons. There is magic in a wayside station which can never be found at a bus-stop, or from getting in and out of the car at your door.

Bungay Station had an isolated position at the bottom of a long slope at the end of Outney Road. It was built in 1860, and the last journey was taken on a very cold January night in 1952. A comparatively short period of time for a place that was of great importance to the town. It must have been of great benefit then, when the only means of transport was a pony cart, if you had one. Most people had to rely on their own strong legs.

It seems on looking back to our younger days that all our summers were long and hot and sunny. So I always think of Bungay railway station standing in a blaze of sunshine. On the dusty road outside, the cab from the King's Head was waiting for passengers, the horse standing patiently, except for an occasional swish of his tail. The bank beside the 'down' platform would be a tangled mass of the yellow Rose of Sharon, seeming to blaze in the sunshine. But the platform could be cold indeed in winter, with an east wind sweeping across the Common, and whistling through the unheated Waiting Rooms.

A stone's throw away, the River Waveney narrow and shallow at this point, flows by. The bridge that spanned it is there no more, but you can still see the rough ends of wood blackened by the smoke from years of passing steam trains (at least, you could until the bridge, and all the remaining station buildings were demolished to make way for the road by-pass completed in 1983). On Saturdays, in summer, and during the long August holiday, the river here was alive with children paddling, and trying to catch the tiny tiddlers in tin buckets, or jam-jars, or even in large handkerchiefs held tightly at the corners. The handkerchief was slipped under a shoal of small fish, and brought out expectantly. There was usually an "Ooh-aah", of disappointment, for the fish had all swum happily away.

There were no pretty sun suits or bathing shorts worn by the paddlers in those days. Thick socks were taken off and rolled up carefully and stuffed inside the leather boots which were placed on the bank. The boys rolled up their knickerbockers above the knee, and the girls held up their rather long skirts, for woe betide if any of them arrived home with the hems of their skirts or the bottoms of their trousers wet and muddy.

I went to the Train Bridge river today, at almost the middle of the school holidays. The river was deserted. The shallow water flowed quietly along, rippling in the sunlight. Round the remains of the old bridge, forget-me-nots were growing, half in, and half out of the water.

And suddenly I saw the river again as it used to be on every warm summer's day, alive with happy, paddling children, gay with their laughter and ecstatic shivery cries as the cold water reached almost to their knees, or an unfortunate tiddler had been caught in the outstretched handkerchief. A sudden click as the train signal fell, and instantly – silence. Then a chorus "Here's the train!" The braver of the paddlers would stand under the bridge, waiting for the train to rush overhead with a great screaming whistle as it approached the station. The more timid ones would splash with hasty steps away from the bridge, or scramble to an elder sister sitting on the bank. For, to tiny tots who had never known the fiendish noises of today's traffic, the train was a frightening monster, belching out hot steam, and grinding to a standstill with an ear-shattering screech!

Passengers waved from the train windows and

the children waved excitedly back. On one occasion an extra long train stopped on the bridge, and waited some minutes before drawing up to the station platform. It was a troop train, full of khaki-clad soldiers. They leaned over the carriage doors, and shouted pleasantries to the children in the water below. Then one of them threw a penny down, and rush of children splashed to retrieve it from the river bed. Then another soldier followed suit, and then another, until there was a shower of pennies from the cheerful young 'Tommies' to the eager waiting hands of the children. A penny was wealth then, for few children had more than one coin a week for pocket money.

But I must return to describing the railway station itself. There was always much activity when a train was due, and for several minutes after it departed. I seem to remember that there were always two porters on duty, trundling luggage trolleys, or milk-churns along the platform. There was much commotion of clucking and cackling if one of the 'parcels' was a crate of hens or ducks!

The Station Master, immaculate in his blue frock coat and peaked hat, stood in the doorway of his office, and the ticket collector hovered between the Waiting Room door and the gate to the road to bar any ticket-shy folk. Platform tickets were never required on Bungay station, so we could meet our friends from the train or see them off again without payment.

A well stocked bookstall stood next to the Waiting Room, a branch of W.H. Smith's. As well as daily papers and periodicals, new books were on display, and there was also a lending library. We used to buy our own favourite magazines there, the 'School Friend', and 'Magnet' of Bessie and Billy Bunter fame.

Each day there were six trains up and six down, but on Sundays the station was as quiet and deserted as the Trainbridge area seems to be now. There were special excursion trains to the seaside on Bank Holidays; and special trains were also provided for the Harleston Show. This was held on August Bank Holiday Monday, when that particular day, the first Monday in August, really was the holiday of the year. It was probably the only free day that working people could get, and was almost as eagerly awaited as Christmas Day. Excursion trains were always packed as whole families set out, children clutching spades and pails, and parents carrying canvas bags containing sandwiches. Good substantial sandwiches of thick slices of ham between thick slices of home-made bread. There was no thin sliced wrapped bread then.

The trippers were very un-seaside-like in their apparel. Indeed, the men wore their Sunday best clothes, a thick serge suit, and stiff collar, and a trilby hat or cloth cap. A straw boater might be seen and perhaps Mama would carry a sunshade.

There must have been dreary, wet August holidays, but in memory I recall only the sunny days, and the surge of excitement as we jerked up and down on the seat of the railway carriage, as the train slowly chugged out of the station.

Yes, the station in its short years of existence

saw many happy comings and goings, and many sad ones too; the bridal party waved off in a shower of confetti, or the sad departure of relatives after a funeral. Friends and relations would be greeted as they arrived to stay for a holiday, and then the mournful wavings of farewell. A yearly visit was often all that could be managed when money was scarce.

"Goodbye, see you next year. Don't forget to write".

"Goodbye, don't forget to tell Grandma to ...".

But what was to be told Grandma was blown away in a rush of steam, as the train puffed under the bridge and away.

CHAPTER TEN

# War Time

The First World War brought far less upheaval to Bungay than that caused by the Second World War. There were no evacuees, or issue of gas masks, and food rationing when it came was not so drastic for people in country districts as it was in larger towns and cities. As I have already written, most householders kept a few chickens, rabbits, or even a pig, and managed to grow vegetables in a small space. On St. Mary's Fields where now stands the High School and housing estates, there were allotments.

On quiet Saturday afternoons in summer you could hear the distant thud of heavy guns as the fighting edged nearer the Channel coast. But it was all so far away and there was no radio to bring the latest news into our homes as it does now. People from Lowestoft came to live with relatives in Bungay for the duration of the war because of possible naval bombardment on the coast. There was no 'black-out' except during zeppelin raids and these were few. One occasionally heard stage whispering in the dark street beneath the bedroom window:–

"Put out that light! There's a raid on". And why everybody spoke in whispers I do not know.

"What is it Mama?" we would call down the stairway. "Why is everybody in the street?"

"It's only a zeppelin going over. Go off to sleep".

"I want to see it! Is it the Pulham Pig?" For we had a zeppelin, almost a local one, which was based at Pulham. We often saw it low in the sky across the Common, a thick nosed long greyish blue object descending very slowly to its base. So slowly that it seemed to be suspended in the sky for hours and we grew tired of watching it.

One Saturday night a bomb was dropped on the Common, and next morning we went with Dadda to see the crater it had made. The most frightening part of the raids was the sound of the baying of the mules from the army camp on the Common. They seemed to sense danger and cried from one to the other with a forlorn sound, half neighing, and half howling. The searchlights also which swept the dark skies with their white arcs of light were frightening too, to a child, seeming to decrease the distance between the sky, with its lurking enemy raider, and our familiar street which suddenly was not friendly terra firma anymore.The military had a camp on the Common and at Flixton Park. A few dispatch riders roared around noisily on 'bone-shaker' motorbikes. Apart from these there was little mechanical transport.

On Saturday mornings the transport wagons, each drawn by four horses or mules came from the Flixton Camp to the Goods Station at Bungay to collect their provisions. A long line of these carts stretched the whole length of Broad Street, across the Market Place, and even into St. Mary's Street. The words 'queue' and 'traffic jams' were not familiar then, but it was indeed a long queue of horses or mules, and transports waiting patiently, on the whole, for their turn to move up a transport length at a time as the vehicle in front got nearer to its turn to be served at the Station. It was not a traffic jam, for everything worked with military precision, the waiting line of carts on the left-hand side of the road and the returning loaded vehicles going back to Flixton on the right.

The animals grew restive sometimes, pawing the ground and tossing their heads and even trying to move a little out of line. On at least two occasions, frightened probably by a train whistle, horses stampeded and raced from the station yard dragging a half-loaded vehicle rattling behind. To see four wildly galloping horses out of control tearing through the narrow street, the cart behind them swaying drunkenly, half overturning, a white-faced driver trying desperately to keep his seat and check the horses, is not a spectacle one forgets very easily.

But the great event of that summer of 1916 was the Review of the Troops at Beccles by King George V. In childhood's memory, summer was always sunny and hot. There was no doubt that this day on which the troops marched from Bungay and Flixton to Beccles was a really hot one, and many of the footsore overladen men must have looked up at the pitiless blue sky hoping to see even one small cloud appear to give a moment's shade. For they marched in full kit, their thick serge khaki uniforms buttoned to the neck, tightly rolled puttees from the knee downward, thick leather boots. They carried their rifles and kitbags and greatcoats, and marched on the dusty open road the seven hot miles to Beccles.

The whole town must have gathered on the pavements round the Market Place to watch the soldiers march through, children waving flags and cheering as if the war had ended and this was a Victory Parade. The rhythmic tramp of marching feet seemed endless. Along St. Mary's Street from the camp at Flixton Park and along Earsham Street from the Common, the rows of steadily moving troops disappeared down Bridge Street. The sun glinted on the well polished brass buttons on their uniforms and on cap badges.

The men at the Camp seemed to spend so much time in 'spit and polish'. Even on Sunday evenings they could be seen sitting outside their tents on upturned buckets polishing away at boots or buttons or badges.

Some of the officers rode on horseback, others marched by the side of the men. Their uniforms, also khaki, seemed to be made of a lighter material than those of their men. Transports were drawn by mules or horses. The transport drivers were the lucky ones, no doubt envied by the footsloggers. This was only the beginning of the march, the men fresh, unwearied, they moved with a beautiful even stride to the stirring music of a brass band. And as they disappeared down Bridge Street and the drum beats faded in the distance, a Scottish regiment came along with its bagpipes and their wailing, haunting music. The lighter step of the players and their neatly swinging kilts was indeed 'poetry in motion'. Yes, this was but the beginning of the march before the heavy uniforms grew heavier with sweat, and the feet must have burned and throbbed agonisingly in the heavy boots, and the caps made a deep red dent across the aching foreheads.

Some of the older children marched behind the soldiers for a mile or so, some of the younger ones tagged behind. A call from the parent "Mind you don't go too far, do your dinner 'ull be cold. I'm not keeping that hot for you". Who wanted steaming suet dumplings and hot savoury stew on such a day?

The crowd quickly drifted away and the pavements outside Wightman's the drapers, and Tom Spalding's the greengrocer, and Mutimer's the grocer, and Jackson's the ironmonger, became empty. A lady assistant from the Post Office at the top of Bridge Street, shooed away some stragglers sitting on the Post Office steps, and the Market Place held nothing but an echo of marching feet, and drum beats and wailing bagpipes, and a small Union Jack lying solitary in the dust.

During the time the Military were stationed here, open air services were held on the Common on fine Sunday evenings. These were usually taken by the Reverend Roger Bulstrode, Vicar of St. Mary's and also Chaplain to the Forces. Whether he was above medium height I do not know, but in his khaki uniform, he looked broad shouldered and strong and very reliable. He was fond of children, and usually had several around him, chatting away. On Saturday afternoons he took parties of school children to the top of St. Mary's church tower. The charge was one penny each, the money being given to one of the war-time charities. The Vicar climbed on ahead, the children scrambling up the winding steps behind him. Every now and then his voice would boom hauntingly from above – "Watch out there for a broken step". The scramble up the dim, dusty stairway and out on to the open tower top, a small circle of sky above, and a panorama of houses, and Common and woodland stretched out beneath, never lost its delight for us.

The open-air services attracted a large crowd. Music for the hymns was provided by a harmonium borrowed from one of the Sunday School rooms, probably from the Mission Hall in Broad Street. It was carried on a small army handcart. There was no lack of volunteers among the boys to push and pull it along. Indeed it often had a very erratic zigzag course to its destination.

Many fathers and sons and sweethearts from the town were serving on the battlefields overseas, so the male voices came from the croaks of the old men, the piping tenor of the boys, and the rich hearty tones of the men at the camp. A favourite hymn at that time, "Christian Seek Not Yet Repose', has a plaintive air which can be dragging and over-mournful in the confines of a church. The harmonium player, followed by the soldiers, gave it an almost galloping gaiety, as they flung it out over the Common at least half a verse ahead of the wailing voices of some of the older ones. In the end, the tremulous tones of the old ladies triumphed, for as the strong masculine voices threw their last challenge "Ambushed lies the evil one", to echo round the trees of Bath Hills, the ladies held the field for several seconds longer with their "Wa-a-a-tch and Pr-aa-y".

The harmonium was placed on some ricketty edifice, and for the sermon, the Vicar climbed up beside it. His head held high, his rich voice, unaided by a loud speaker, rose and fell in the evening air. Occasionally there was a soft lowing from the cattle on the marshes or a mule might bay suddenly. There was a very large dog at the camp, a Great Dane, very fearsome looking to unwarranted callers, but indeed he was good natured and gentle, and most of the children loved him. At these open air services, he was usually stretched out on the grass in front of the congregation, his heavy jowl resting on his huge paws. He occasionally turned his rather blood-shot eyes heavenward, no doubt petitioning the Almighty in his own fashion.

I cannot tell you the text or the theme of any of the sermons. It was 'grown-up' matter, and to children held less meaning than the wind, rustling through the poplars or the river rushing over the stones at Train Bridge. Children plucked sleepily at the sorrel in the grass beside them and chewed the sharp tasting acidy leaves. The evening air became a little chilly and the pink sunset light lingered in sinister fashion on the dark red patches of sorrel. One shivered a little and leaned against Dada, and whispered, "Please can we go home now?" for it was past our usual bedtime. Mama would whisper "You take the children. I will stay for the last hymn."

As we walked towards home the searchlights would already begin to sweep the evening sky with their questing arcs of light.

In the windows of Short's, the Newsagents were many picture-postcards especially for 'Our Tommies at the Front'. Pictures of khaki-clad young men resting in the trenches. Shafts of light more golden than sunlight beaming from the sky on to their sleeping faces. "Lead Kindly Light" was the caption. Or a soldier resting his head on his haversack, and his hands reaching up to what looked like a ladder, its top disappearing into gold-lit fleecy clouds. "Nearer My God To Thee", printed underneath. There were also the 'comic' postcards depicting the British sense of humour shining through the misery of trench warfare. No doubt these gave homesick young men more of a lift than did the 'Holy, Holy' ones.

The searchlights were not so alarming in this half light of evening as they were in the black of night when we peeped fearfully from the bedroom window, and saw them suddenly light up the sky, engulfing it in a light stronger than moonlight. And suddenly they would be switched off, leaving a more intense darkness than before. The evening searchlights made one think sleepily of Jacob's Ladder and the angels ascending and descending.

And so, home to a glass of cold milk, fresh and creamy, and a sense of well-being when you were kissed and tucked up in bed and the room was filled with that sense of peace that passes all understanding and which is rarely found again when childhood is passed.

During the Septembers and Octobers of 1917 and 1918, schoolchildren were given half-day holidays to gather blackberries and acorns to help the War-effort. The blackberries were sent to factories for jam for the troops, and the acorns used for some sort of fodder for cattle. I do not remember ever being told at that time that acorns are poisonous. The boys used them as ammunition for their pop-guns, biting each acorn in half and pressing it hard into the barrel of the pop-gun which was made from a piece of elder with the pith wedged out.

It was expected but not compulsory for the blackberries and acorns to be taken to school. They were weighed and the gatherer was given a penny a pound for the blackberries. I expect many of the mothers were glad to keep this fruit for their own use. Indeed it was the custom for the whole family to spend an afternoon blackberrying, carrying baskets and metal cans and a walking stick for pulling down the blackest shiniest berries which always seemed to be on the highest branch. On looking back, those September blackberrying expeditions were indeed days of "mellow fruitfulness". The smell of blackberries on our stained and scratched hands and the taste of berries on our lips was warm and memorable. After the 30th of September all brambles were left alone, for after that date they belonged to the Devil and became soggy and tasteless. On misty October mornings they are usually garlanded with silvery webs with a large fat spider in the centre of each. And who would dare to reach past his eight horrible legs for the sake of an inedible fruit?

Constitution Hill was an excellent place for blackberrying. Hedges far from the road, so the berries were free of dust. Now, with the pitiful destruction of so many beautiful hedges, the rich harvest of berries is destroyed also.

Gleaning was another most enjoyable way of spending a September afternoon. After the reaping was finished by the farmer and his labourers, there were still broken heads of corn scattered on the ground. These were very useful at a time when most families kept a few chickens. It was a delight to walk across the stubble fields, the hedges around beautiful with the shining red rosehips and dark red haw berries entangled in a wealth of Old Man's Beard.

I am always full of gratitude that so much of my life has been spent in our lovely Suffolk countryside, where every season has something new to offer. The games season of bowling hoops, spinning tops, marbles, and skipping; then picking primoses in Shoe Devil Lane, gathering acorns and blackberries, paddling in the Train Bridge river, gleaning corn, and, perhaps the happiest of all, trundling a barrow to find holly – holly with many berries and one special piece to stick in the Christmas pudding. St. Valentine's Eve, and Guy Fawkes, and carol singing. There was always something to enjoy, something to look forward to, and, even in childhood, a happy looking back.

"Let's go and get primroses, remember the lovely ones we gathered last year? Near the stream. There were tadpoles and little frogs. Do you remember?"